Pat Robie

To help keep you occupied at least for
an hour... It was supposed to arrive for
your birthday, but they had to backorder.
I've enjoyed his essays in New Yorker for
years... hope you do, too.

Pat

Israel Shenker

Harmless
Drudges

Wizards of Language—
ancient, medieval and modern

Barnhart Books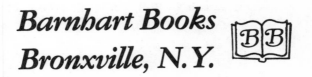
Bronxville, N.Y.

Many pieces in this book appeared, in different form, in *THE NEW YORK TIMES:* © 1968, 1969, 1970, 1972, 1973, 1974, 1975, 1976, 1977, 1978 by THE NEW YORK TIMES COMPANY. Reprinted by permission.

INSULT DICTIONARY © 1966, by TIME, Inc. Reprinted by permission.

ERIC PARTRIDGE © 1974, by SATURDAY REVIEW. Reprinted by permission.

Several pieces appeared in WORDS AND THEIR MASTERS © 1974 by DOUBLEDAY.

FOR JENNIE LESCHES,

who merits a dictionary's best words

Contents

PREFACE   *7*

WORDS AND THEIR WATCHERS   *11*

The Language of Politics • The Great Society Dictionary
Briticisms • Insults

SHADES OF MEANING   *29*

Ghost Words • Housewife

EXOTIC TONGUES   *37*

A Gaggle of Dictionaries • French and English • Estonian
Ladino • Six Thousand Dictionaries • Joys of Yiddish

THE BRITISH   *71*

A British Concise Dictionary Editor • A R Babcock • Oxford
English Dictionary • Oxford Dictionary of English Proverbs

THE AMERICANS   *99*

Webster's New Collegiate Dictionary • Thesaurus

CLERKS TO THE LANGUAGE   *113*

Eric Partridge • Clarence Barnhart • Noah Webster
Middle English Dictionary

FASHIONS OF USAGE   *139*

American Heritage Dictionary—I • American Heritage
Dictionary—II • Harper Dictionary of Contemporary
Usage

PREFACE

To determine why one becomes fascinated with words demands uncommon acumen, and I plead innocent of any such excess. But I know precisely where and when I set forth to trail the harmless drudge to his lair. In 1966, to escape the heat of summer in Rome, where I was based as a correspondent for *Time*, I went to work in the magazine's London bureau. A newspaper article about a local insult dictionary set my palate quivering, and I tracked down the vituperative lexicographer for samples of his art.

My appetite was whetted, but it took the Soviet invasion of Czechoslovakia to allow me a second taste. By then—August of 1968—I was about to come to New York to work for *The New York Times*. The foreign editor phoned me in London (once more it was hot in Rome) and asked me to go to work right away. He told me to head for Hungary and report reaction to the Czech crisis.

Lexicography was far from my mind and I was at a loss for words when plainclothes police woke me at my hotel in Budapest, escorted me to a train, kept me under surveillance en route to the border, and finally expelled me. My crime—it was never specified for me, either in Hungarian or any other language—must have been that I was working as a reporter while on a tourist visa. When I finally arrived in Vienna, shaken by the experience, I cabled the foreign editor that I was safe in Austria after having been arrested and expelled. Naturally I expected him to reply that I had performed nobly in the cause of a free press, and that I would go down in the annals of journalism. His answering cable read: "TRY BULGARIA."

There I was, two days later, sitting in Sofia, fresh to the country and trembling every time I remembered that I was a recidivist, once more traveling on a tourist visa. The first day I scurried around and put together a report on how Bulgaria was reacting to the affair of Czechoslovakia. The second day brought the usual dilemma of the foreign correspondent—what to say on the second day of a visit to a new country. Close to despair, I decided to visit the local synagogue to see if there were any miracles available. I found Isaac Moscona, who was acting as caretaker and who had little to say about the Soviet Union but lots to say about the local Jewish vernacular. He had just completed a Ladino-Bulgarian dictionary—a triumph for him, a subject for me.

When I finally reached New York without benefit of further arrest or expulsion, I made it my pleasure to find other miracle-workers of lexicography—professional, amateur, and something in between, working on dictionaries modern, medieval and ancient. My weakness for the breed was such that editors of *The Times*, bent on saving my soul, labored to make me ignore word-lists and return occasion-

Preface

ally to less esoteric pursuit. Since they were unprepared to have me arrested or expelled, I ignored their pleas and went my way. Indulgently, they finally resigned themselves to letting me have freedom on the trail and space in the paper. This book is the product of that indulgence.

Israel Shenker

New York City
1979

WORDS AND
THEIR WATCHERS

The Language of
Politics

As one of President Nixon's speechwriters, William Safire had only the ghost of a chance of emerging from the shadow of his alter ego. But as the author of *The New Language of Politics—A Dictionary of Catchwords, Slogans & Political Usage* he tasted the joys of un-altered ego.

He began noting the waxing and waning phrases of politics, in 1966, on a moonlight basis, while working as a New York public relations man. When the first edition emerged into the sunlight in 1968, there were about 1,000 entries and 350,000 words. "It's still in print," said the author, "but a stampede there isn't."

The second edition (Collier Books, $4.95, paper) had about 1,200 entries, 400,000 words, and evidence of revisionist scholarship.

"Everything I do is partisan—except lexicography," Mr. Safire said. "The long hand of Dr. Samuel Johnson reaches out and stays you from partisanship. I try to be scrupulous."

Inside the Administration is a good place for a lexicographer: he can ask associates when they first used *game plan*, send Defense Department officials scurrying to find the initial use of *Vietnamization*, or help newsmen prepare *ticktocks* (chronicle chronology) and *thumbsuckers* (think pieces).

"The language of politics is a language of excess, of color and vivid exaggerations," said Mr. Safire. "From the very beginning an instinct for the jugular—which is an image of a wolf going for another wolf's throat—is a standard political Americanism, meaning a tough-mindedness or a willingness to engage in political combat. Because it's so extreme it has a nice ludicrous overtone that takes the edge off the fury of the phrase.

"Good political language fills a void. *Iron Curtain*. Perfect example. As subsequent research showed, Joe Goebbels and 40 other people used it before Churchill, but Churchill popularized it.

"Sometimes political language springs into being. For example a word that I omitted in this edition, but that belongs there, is *hardhat*. I have *Middle American*, I have *heartland*, I have *forgotten American* and *silent majority*.

"*Silent Majority* is brilliant political language. Oddly, the President was not trying to make a phrase. He didn't capitalize *silent majority* in the course of the speech, nor did he expect it to be picked out as a key line."

Some phrases resulted from *boosting*—adding irony or new meaning to a familiar phrase. *Knee-jerk liberal* was brought up to date with *limousine liberal*, and Lyndon Johnson took John Kennedy's "let us begin" and said "let us continue."

Mr. Safire cited what he termed "beautiful phrases"— "just and lasting peace," "lift of a driving dream." "Phrases like those are often derided as cornball or an attempt at eloquence," he said. "But you have to have an attempt at eloquence to have eloquence. 'Four score and seven years ago' can be derided as a labored effort to add class and solemnity to '87.' But it works."

Bad political language is *bloviation,* a word Mr. Safire credits to President Harding, whom he also cites as the source for *normalcy* and *Founding Fathers* (an expression which has been boosted to "Fondling Fathers"). "To *bloviate* is to talk meaninglessly," said Mr. Safire. "The kind of thing Coolidge never did."

"Political language can be used to obfuscate and confuse, just as it can be used to eloquently uplift. It can be used to draw 'red herrings' across the trail and vilify and subject people to a 'hail of dead cats'—which is one of my favorite phrases."

Sometimes a great phrase appears to emerge full-blown, if not full-bloviated, from a candidate's mind. "Muskie must have done it when he said 'Now is the time for a *new beginning.*' " said Mr. Safire.

"Right? He thought to himself *New Deal, New Frontier, Great Society, New Beginning. New Beginning* we used for Nixon; I think the President used it in the 1970 State of the Union. *New Departure* is another. It goes way back in American history. That's not to be derisive about it. There are 50 good thematic, beginning-type phrases like that which one consciously selects."

The first edition of the dictionary helped candidate Nixon produce variations on a theme in his acceptance speech at the 1968 Miami convention. When Mr. Nixon wanted to use the "I see" construction, Mr. Safire showed him previous employment by Franklin D. Roosevelt, Adlai E. Stevenson and others.

"I had about six different 'I see's,' so he was able to

review them and then come up with his own." With his vision corrected, Mr. Nixon declared: "'I see' a day when the President of the United States is respected...'I see' a day when our 'senior citizens' and millions of others can plan for the future..."

How was President Nixon at political language? "Brilliant" said Mr. Safire. "He's tops... That 'lift of a driving dream.' The 'generation of peace.' The 'New Prosperity.' 'Prosperity without inflation and without war.' Those phrases are simple, direct, gutty, understandable, gripping.

"As soon as he saw 'Let me make one thing perfectly clear' being parodied, he stopped. Like John Kennedy's 'vigah' or Johnson's 'continyuh'—as soon as it becomes a cliché you move off it."

One critic complained that the first edition omitted 'You won't have Nixon to kick around any more.' "It's not part of the language," said Mr. Safire. "It's a good...it's a familiar quote. But what word or phrase is in it?"

Shouldn't 'used-car salesman' be in the dictionary? "I could see that," he said, and acknowledged that a few other possibles were missing: *busing, genocide, ghetto, Little Red Book* ("Yeah, I guess so, right before *Little Tin Box*"), *ethnics, quality education* ("In the category of words that have been accused of being *code words*"), *reverse quotas* ("I would have that under *reverse bigotry*").

Some words he refused to admit: "*Women's Lip* (Oh God, did I get mail: Ever since I used it I've been very cautious with my treatment of Women's Lib...eration ...Movement), *incursion* (a one-week wonder), *Phase Two* (By the third edition we'll be in *Phase 12*, and people will forget the phases) and *crisis* ('Concern!' 'Concern!' We never use the word 'crisis')."

For moving, politically memorable speaking, a Safire favorite was Spiro Agnew. "He's done more in the way of coinages than anybody since Harold Ickes and John Foster Dulles," the lexicographer said. "*Instant analysis. Effete snobs. Household word. Nattering nabobs of negativism.*"

Mr. Safire noted that Mr. Agnew credited him with *nattering nabobs*, an admission violating the "Code of the Hills," which prohibits speechwriters claiming credit for coinages in this realm.

Vice President Agnew expressed his appreciation of Mr. Safire's treatment of such matters by inscribing a photo "to a great 'wordsmith.'" That tribute proved to be an embarrassment of niches, for Mr. Safire's first edition defined *wordsmith* as a "hack ghostwriter." "The mildest kind of *blooper*, a half-gaffe," said Mr. Safire, whose dictionary defines *blooper* as "worse than a *goof*, more adult than a *boo-boo*, not as serious as a *blunder*, equivalent to a *gaffe*." The second edition has not changed its definition of *wordsmith*, but Mr. Safire insists that the word has now lost its pejorative connotation.

The *wordsmith*-lexicographer delights in his brighter definitions. "I usually slump back in my seat and sort of play the tape over and over and listen to it," he said. "For example, my definition in the book of *Silent Majority*—'the remarkable legion of the unremarked.' I kind of like that. You read it in the typewriter, then you wait and see it in type and you read it there and then occasionally, when nobody's looking, you turn back to that page. You let your friends draw it out of you. You go through the Jimmy Stewart routine: you look down at the ground and you dig your toe in the carpet and you kind of move it around and murmur 'Aw, shucks!'"

The Great Society Dictionary

The Great Society Dictionary begins with indignation and ends with *zap* ("to shoot down in cold blood, especially a Gook"). Its inevitable sequel, *The Great Imperial Dictionary*, takes the world for its province.

Author of both is Professor Edward S. Herman, who teaches finance at the University of Pennsylvania's Wharton School of Finance and Commerce. Inspired by Ambrose Bierce's *Devil's Dictionary*, he worked on the books for five years, in lulls between fits of rage.

"The linguistic convulsions inspired by Vietnam have been fundamental," Professor Herman said.

Vietcong, for example, he translates as "a Vietnamese peasant, especially one that we have killed." Following the definition is a note: "see *enemy structure*." In proper alphabetical sequence this is defined as "a thatched hut that we destroy." Once more a note is appended: "see *home*." *Home* is defined as "a thatched hut that they destroy."

Infiltration is "their movement of troops into the battle zone"; *reinforcement* is "our movement of troops into the battle zone." *Aggression* is "providing aid and comfort to the side that we oppose," and *assistance* is "providing aid and *comfort to the side that we favor." Defensive* is "our move," *offensive* is "their move." *Atrocities* are their killings, *retaliations* are ours. *Interrogation* is "torture," *neutralize* is "kill." *Hard-boiled* emerges as "cold-blooded, possessing fortitude in bearing with the sufferings of others." *Dove* is "one who favors the last escalation but is opposed to the next." *Negotiations* are "the process of accepting the surrender of the ill-gotten gains of the enemy." *Patience* is "acquiescence." *Peace with honor* equals "victory," and *victory* is "annihilation." *A century of peace* is "hundred proof moonshine."

Professor Herman's dictionaries leave Vietnam to consider imperial canons large and small. *Faith* is put down as "my deeply held belief," *fanaticism* as "his deeply held belief." *Pledge* is defined as "a solemn political promise based on the public's short memory." *Self-determination* is defined as "the right of a people to select a government acceptable to us," and *calculated risk* is simply "an incalculable risk." *Anti-ballistic missile* is brought down to earth as "an expensive cure for which there is no disease." *Armaggedon* is "a plausible scenario," *defeat* is "an implausible scenario." *Military-industrial complex* is "the Pentagon and its Hundred Neediest Cases."

Right at home, Professor Herman finds equally broad targets. *Conservatism* is "an ideology which holds that Government is too big except for the police and army." *Anarchy* is "rapid, unfamiliar change not beneficial to my interests." *March, protest,* is "riot, incitement to." *Coddling* is "reliance on due process of law." *Riot* is "a deplorable outburst of violence by the inhabitants of the cracks in the floor of the Great Society." *Urban renewal* is "Negro removal."

Professor Herman has been dividing his time between

pursuing the acceptable and decrying the unthinkable. He is an expert on banking, monopoly and competition, co-author of the textbook *Money and Banking: Analysis and Policy*, and author of *Atrocities in Vietnam: Myths and Realities*. As befits the academic in him, he has enriched his dictionaries with an apparatus of scholarly footnotes. Many who escape the barbs of his definitions get their come-downance there.

Having omitted any reference to Spiro Agnew, Professor Herman felt confident that Mr. Agnew would find a place in the foot-in-mouth notes of a revised dictionary. Walt W. Rostow, a presidential aide closely identified with the Johnson administration's Vietnam policy, was also omitted, but he seems doomed to permanent obscurity. Professor Herman explained: "Rostow is out because I lose my temper every time I think of him." Joseph Alsop, the columnist, was included, however, in *Alsop's Fables*—"Tales written to supply the official demand for imperial myths."

To supply the unofficial demand for his dictionaries, copies were printed to sell at one dollar, with proceeds going to The Philadelphia Resistance, an organization which opposed the war in Vietnam. Professor Herman considered the price a reasonable sum, no relation of course to *acceptable cost*—the first term defined in his Great Society Dictionary ("in nuclear chicken theory, a number of megadeaths within the limit defining a feasible nuclear strategy").

Briticisms

Americans and British are close in many ways, but words apart.

George Bernard Shaw spoke of Britain and America as two countries divided by a common tongue. The Welsh poet, Dylan Thomas, visiting America, complained that he was "up against the barrier of a common language."

East may be East and West West, but men on both sides of New York's Fifth Avenue are trying to simplify the division and pierce the barrier.

In his functional aerie at Columbia University, Professor Allen Walker Read worked forty years on a dictionary of English used in England but not in America, to be titled *A Dictionary of the English of England.*

In a plush office at 1 East 44th Street, Norman W. Schur, a worldly attorney who practices in Britain as well as in America, completed his five-year, labor-of-love guide to the linguistically perplexed, called *British-Self-Taught (With Comments in American).*

Both men revel in the diversity of the somewhat common tongue, and delight in specifics: English *biscuit* for American *cookie, char* and *daily* for *maid, cutting* for *clipping, flat* for *apartment, lift* for *elevator, wretched* for *awful* or simply *terrible.*

From A to Z, American English and English English are abuzz with differences. The British call *Z zed. Zero* comes to *naught, nought* or just plain *cipher,* while a *duck* in English scoring is reduced to a *goose egg* on American turf.

There is a pronounced difference that reaches beyond class or accent. The word *schedule* is pronounced "shedule" in England. A *lieutenant* in America is called "leftenant" across the Atlantic.

International spelling bees would be painfully confused between *honor—honour, curb—kerb, defense—defence, check—cheque, jail—gaol, tire—tyre.* American English stubbornly prefers a single *l* in *traveler* and *marvelous.* But when the British travel light (*fulfil, instal, instil*) Americans get their fill: *install, instill.*

The English, as Mr. Schur points out, are not always given to understatement, and thus speak of *sailing boat, rowing boat, washing day, cookery book, iced water, wheeled chair, twin-bedded room* and *two-roomed flat.* But while the English make do with *spring-clean,* Americans are forever insisting on *spring-cleaning.* Speech west of the Atlantic often belabors the obvious, while British is content to labour it. An American would say: "Lie down and get rested up," while the Briton would wind up *rested.*

Americans are chary about diphthongs—thus writing *esthete* (not *aesthete*) and *ecumenical* (not *oecumenical*). The view of collective bodies is equally singular here (Harvard plays Yale), not there (Oxford play Cambridge).

In a study entitled *American into English,* G.V. Carey, a British proofreader and stylist, argued that even the hyphen was often by-passed when English passed into American. He wrote that "American tends to cold-shoulder—or, as they would probably write it, to *cold shoulder*, if not to coldshoulder—the hyphen." He suggested that this could lead to difficulties, as in "His face turned an ugly brick red."

The two peoples not only say different things, or the same things differently, they do them differently as well. "Have a seat," one is told in America, but in Britain "Take a seat." Americans pass people on the street, British pass them in the street. An American fills out forms, a Briton fills them in. The proper Englishman hunts foxes and deer but shoots game birds and rabbits. Americans hunt quail.

S. Gorley Putt, the author, memorialized "English Speaking Disunion," and Robert Knittel, a British publishing executive, said that "Halfway across the ocean our two languages nuzzle up to each other and fraternize enough to become 'mid-Atlinguish.'" Winston Churchill, who dreamed of common nationality for Americans and British, noted that during World War II there had been "long and even acrimonious argument" when both sides—had they only understood each other—really agreed.

The British tread delicately. A *ladybug* in American is a *ladybird* in British. Britons would never eat crow, but they might sample humble pie. "You tell 'em!" an American might exclaim; a Briton would call out "Hear! Hear!" Professor Read suggests that originally this may have been "Hear him! Hear him!" An American, as Mr. Schur notes, "knocks 'em dead," while an Englishman is content to "knock for six."

There is confusion even within the confines of the nominally United Kingdom. Asked Professor Read: "How does one differentiate between an old bean, a gent, a bloke, a chap, a cad, a toff, a lad? What is the exact tone of words like boffin, buffer, duffer, card, flanneled fool, silly ass, heavy swell, brick, masher, bounder, thruster?"

Professor Read would be happy with the services of a P.G. Wodehouse, by which he means of course *the* P.G. Wodehouse. Even the definite article poses problems.

"I think that the word 'the' has enough differences that it should be treated," said Professor Read, and offered literary witness. In *Miss Bax of the Embassy*, Emily Bax asks: "When is a Lady The Lady and when is she only A Lady?" "Costs me the hell of a lot of money," says a (the?) protagonist of *Room at the Top*.

An Englishman will study not law but *the* law, and if he is low on the social ladder he may speak of *the wife* rather than *my wife*. On March *the* first he will drive down *the* High Street to hospital. In *An Anglo-American Interpreter*, H.W. Horwill suggested that an American taken ill in a London street might die before he could make himself understood.

Where but in England could there be a Captain the Lord Louis Mountbatten, a royalty with *savoir-dire* sufficient to pose his candidature (candidacy), as he did in World War II, for the post of Anglo-American interpreter?

Sometimes problems appear forbidding. "It's terribly hard to determine when British expressions became naturalized in America," noted Professor Read, and added: "The very word *American* doesn't connote in England precisely what it does here."

To the British ear *American* has long borne a suggestion of barbarian; *un-American* sounds much more wholesome. About 70 years ago the essayist Samuel McChord Crothers said that *American* implied undoubted excellence only when used in connection (*connexion*) with dentists.

When the theologian Ronald Knox met a group of American advertising men, he expressed shock over their talk of ads for religion, exclaiming: "How vulgar, how American, how almost blasphemous!"

Evelyn Waugh, biographer of Monsignor Knox, wrote to Nancy Mitford that "American polite vocabulary is very different from ours...[it] is pulverized between two stones, refinement and overstatement."

In his introduction to *The Loved One*, Mr. Waugh acknowledged the worst in writing: "My thanks are due...to Mrs. Reginald Allen who corrected my American; to Mr. Cyril Connolly who corrected my English."

American authors must sometimes pay a translation fee for English editions, or at least consent to "anglicization." Mr. Schur, in his legal person, represented an author when the English edition changed words without that author's consent: *maybe* became *perhaps, rock stone, package parcel.*

When Damon Runyon was eased into British English, the publisher provided a glossary, and in it *old tomato* was translated as *loose woman.*

Tomayto tomahto, potayto potahto, getting the meat and veg. into print will take Professor Read years more of work. *A Dictionary of the English of England* will be rich with the apparatus of scholarship, including over 50,000 citations.

Professor Read, who grew up in remote Iowa, came to British as a Rhodes Scholar, and he now speaks what he calls Academic English. Mr. Schur is a word buff who reads grammar on international trains and studiously avoids legalese. "My wife and I were independently anglophile," he said, "and when we met we were off to the races, or as the English would say, 'off to a flying start.' "

Neither the professor nor the lawyer believes there is any chance of Briticisms and Americanisms dividing the language completely. Professor Read says the tie was cast when steamboat travel between the two countries began. "But I'm not in favor of uniformity," he said. "Diversity over the English-speaking world is something to be cultivated.

"The English language exists in a set of branches. There's a dictionary of Canadianisms, another of Jamaican English, someone's working on a dictionary of Indian English, there's talk of a dictionary of Australianisms, and there's been an announcement of a dictionary of South Africanisms.

"Is there such a thing as Philippine English? One Fulbright professor went to Ceylon and he claims there is a Ceylon English, but that may be going too far."

Insults

Peter Wolfe ordered soup in an Italian restaurant in New York, and the waiter had his thumb in it. "It suddenly struck me," said Wolfe, "how useful it would be to tell him in Italian: 'Get your fat thumb out of the soup.' "

There is a sheep in Wolfe's clothing, so he sent the soup back wordlessly. But he got right to work on *The Insult Dictionary*. Here, in five languages—English, French, Spanish, Italian and German—are the appropriate waiter-demanding, soup-straining words of nasty disdain. It has just about every verbally offensive weapon except "Sam, you made the pants too long."

Since Wolfe is a London publisher, it was no trick at all to get Anglo-Saxon insults translated, and he published them himself. The Spanish came from a Spaniard in Spain, the German from a German journalist in London, and the Italian and French from natives who work for the BBC in London. Some of the translations were cruder than the originals: the Frenchman took passable *muck* and turned it into outright *merde*.

The first printing was 30,000 copies, and at five shillings (then 60 cents) a throw the edition was a sellout. A second printing of 20,000 followed, then 30,000 more in time for the height of the tourist indignities. The book sold especially well at airports and railroad stations and was a favorite with students and Americans terrified at the prospect of speechlessness in foreign mire. "I'm convinced most people are not going to use the insults," said Wolfe, "but will come back from a vacation and boast that they did."

Wolfe himself is a rare edition who was born in Transylvania and given a birth certificate printed in Rumanian and handwritten in Hungarian. At the age of three months he was brought to England, and now he speaks fluent Hungarian with the vocabulary of a five-year old. He entered publishing as an office boy, and four years later began publishing on his own. "I publish books that amuse me," he said, "which tell you not what to do but how to put it right if you've done it."

Building on the success of insults, Wolfe prepared the successor to *The Insult Dictionary*—a *Lover's Dictionary*—in time for the Christmas trade. "It's rather warm," goes a typical ice-breaker. "May I take my jacket off?" Before he even knows where the hangers are, he asks, "What time does your husband return?" If the lady proves difficult, he warns, "I'm a customs officer and I believe you're hiding contraband on your person." As she struggles to demonstrate her innocence, he adds, "How do you unfasten these things?... Don't be shy, think of me like a doctor."

In this era of ecumenical largesse, one section is reserved for church lovers. In reverential tones the religious maniac is expected to say "Let's rub hymn books," "I'm a sinner, will you help save me?" and "I'm sorry, my knee slipped from the hassock."

SHADES OF MEANING

Ghost Words

When the Modern Language Association gathered in New York for its 91st annual convention, there was no end of words to mark the occasion—words in English, words in tongues alien, words in earnest, words in jest.

Allen Walker Read, emeritus professor of English from Columbia University, a solidly built man who looks as though he would not countenance anything he could not see or hear, turned up to deal with shadow instead of substance. His subject was ghost words—which dictionaries have a devilish time exorcising.

Not "Boo!" or "I am the ghost of Christmas past," but words that rise from the disordered imagination of writers or editors or the blunders of printers or scribes. "They have no real entity," a distinguished philologist insisted, 90 years ago, and Professor Read called them "evanescent words, commonly regarded as not being 'parts of the language.'"

The best-known, he said, are "nonce words," made up by someone "who feels at home with the formative practices of the language." Algernon Swinburne in 1893 referred to *Oxonolatry*—worship of Oxford. Bardolatry is even more firmly established for worship of Shakespeare, to say less of Brigitte Bardot.

Professor Read also distinguished the closely related "individualism," minted to fill the speaker's need. Diana Trilling, comparing herself with her late husband, said that she was "a less-educated eclectic," and explained, "I don't have as many things to eclect from."

Then there are "hothouse words," a term planted 50 years ago to describe curious artifacsimiles in early English dictionaries. Take *dentiloquent*, speaking through the teeth, *capiloquent*, talking through one's hat, *doctiloquent*, speaking learnedly, and *diffibulate*, to unbutton. They reek of erudition. Some are coined specifically with designs on lexicographic immortality.

Professor Read described a whole ghostly series as "physiological words," words of plain meaning (*uh-huh, yeah, nope, tsk*) and words that take the breath away (*oof, oops*).

When the Oxford English Dictionary was plowing through the language, last century, its editor took pains to justify omission of *abacot*, usually defined—even illustrated—as "the cap of state formerly used by English kings." The word descended by a cascade of blunders from *bicocket*, misprinted *abococket*, altered to *abococke* and finally polished off as *abacot*, perhaps through *abacoc*.

Professor Read gave special pride of place to *dord*, present in the Merriam-Webster 2nd edition of 1934, defined as "density." It began as a slip in an abbreviation file reading "D or d," meaning a capital *D* or a small *d*—for "density." A deletion was ordered in 1940, but in successor dictionaries the ghost went right on walking, too hardy to dispatch.

Predictably enough, elusive words and figures of speech pursue Professor Read even into his sleeping hours. From his dreams he has recorded such nocturnal visitors as *altertrucose, fibricate, possotoficity, spicamento* and *thudinous.* He insisted that his somneologisms "have a definite social context in the experience of the person who did the dreaming."

In the very text of his talk, Professor Read inadvertently created a new ghost of his waking hours, and it will doubtless be henceforth hallowed, haunting dictionaries for years to come. It is the word *owrds,* in a phrase alluding to "the richest harvest of ghost owrds."

That should reassure those whose spirits are willing but whose learning is weak: even an expert like Professor Read occasionally comes a cropper. As he suggested and demonstrated, the infallible way to deal with ghosts is to accept them and use them. They thus win a body of favor.

Housewife

In dictionaries *housewife* is not finding it easy to change her spots.

Consulted for their views on housewife's place, the editors of leading English-language dictionaries have expressed sympathy for the plaint of women liberationists that the housewife's role is less fulfilling than her husband's, and that *housewife* is demeaning, close to a confession, far from a comfort. But the editors opted for keeping the word around—between housewarming and housewifely—until life or liberation provides a satisfactory substitute.

"We have no plans to make any change in the definition," said H. Bosley Woolf, Editorial Director, Dictionaries, for G. & C. Merriam, publishers of *Webster's Third New International* and the *Webster's Seventh New Collegiate*. "It's been in the language since the 13th century, and the objections would be not really to the word but to the profession that the word signifies."

"I don't think the word is sufficiently opprobrious to most people to warrant a change at this period," noted

Herbert A. Gilbert, editor of the Funk & Wagnalls dictionaries, "though we have to look at the evidence. The complaint is about the last part of the definition—'who does not work for a living.' If we do suggest a change in our next edition, it would be to saying 'who is not gainfully employed.' "

Peter L. Davies, executive editor of *The American Heritage Dictionary*, pointed out that in origin the word wife doesn't mean married woman but simply woman—and *housewife* is an exact counterpart of *husband* which means house man. *Housewife* gave birth to the variant *hussy*, but now the two usually keep their distance.

"I've been trying to project what would happen in the future," said Mr. Davies, "and I've failed. I can't see any particular change we would make at the moment. I share the feeling that possibly these things are in a state of flux, and it's too early to see where they're going."

Reached by phone in Oxford, England, Robert W. Burchfield, editor of the *Oxford English Dictionary* supplement, noted: "We had a national census taken a year ago, and some housewives objected to being called that. This wouldn't affect our definition. We would simply have *housewife* in its traditional meaning. But we will react positively to the women's liberation movement, and if they have an alternative, we'll consider it."

In past years, there have been many substitutes proposed and rejected: homemaker, home manager, household executive, household engineer, domestic engineer, domestic economist, even female mistress.

Jess Stein, editor-in-chief of *The Random House Dictionary*, did not give up. "If a new word has to be found, it will have to be sexless, something like 'the-one-who-stays-home-and-runs-the-house' kind of thing," he said.

Mr. Stein then proceeded to suggest a few random thoughts: "*Householder* doesn't signify male or female, but I imagine it's too legalistic. If you invent something like 'co-master of the house,' they'd say why not *co-mistress?*

"I suppose Hugh Hefner has loused up *housemate* with *playmate*. But we have *poet-in-residence* and *artist-in-residence*. Why not *mate-in-residence?*"

"Maybe we should have a word like *houser*," suggested Mr. Stein, and then immediately agreed that it sounded like a German dog.

"You couldn't say the 'in-house worker' and the 'out-house worker,'" he noted.

House made him think of the French "maison," which, he admitted, would make *housewife* "maisonette." What about using Latin, he wondered, where "domus" means house? A man could be the "domino," a woman the "domina," and they could fight it out for domination.

Returning to English, he pondered the possibilities from *bungalow*—namely, *bungler* for the male and *bungla* for the woman, but that was too political-sounding.

Proceeding directly into English English, and poaching on the reserve of Mr. Burchfield, Mr. Stein wondered what lexicographers could do if they started from *flat*—the Anglo-Saxon word for apartment. What woman could possibly resist flattery?

EXOTIC TONGUES

A Gaggle of
Dictionaries

At the University of Chicago's Oriental Institute, scholarship is often esoteric, dealing with civilizations long deceased. But they all left their marks, which ingenious specialists seek to master. To help others as well as themselves, the institute's linguists are laboring at a gaggle of dictionaries of ancient languages, and even one dictionary for a contemporary language, since it may illuminate extinct predecessors.

— — —

The *Chicago Assyrian Dictionary* project, which grapples with a language written from about 2600 B.C. to A.D. 100, may itself qualify as ancient. Work began in 1921, the first volume emerged in 1956, the 14th in 1977, and the world may be shuddering at the gates of 1984 before CAD reaches an honorable conclusion.

Professor Erica Reiner, the present editor, has been at it 25 years, and she is pleased that Westerners now speak of culture going back not to Greece but to Mesopotamia. Assyrian, more commonly known as Akkadian, was spoken in the land between the Tigris and the Euphrates; it was in cuneiform—wedge-shaped letters, impressed by stylus on clay or wax or incised on stone, that the fruits of early civilization were handed round.

"Thousands of new tablets are dug up all the time," Dr. Renee Gallery, a staff member, said. "Books written 20 years ago are often obsolete. The thing that bothered me about Old Testament—which used to be my field—was tramping over the same old topics year after year."

There is a large body of texts, many afflicted with contemporary concerns: "What I feared has happened—I am pregnant." Other passages are tinged with unworldly purple: "Kasuski na-ad-ru kima irra gardamu lisabriq"— "May your raging weapon strike the evil with lightning like the plague-god."

Professor Reiner, now busy on *Q*, is inclined to believe that whatever letter she is working on is the hardest. Benno Landsberger, a former editor of CAD, used to say about any word on which he was consulted, "This is the most difficult word in the language."

A common Akkadian verb like *epesu* can delay the dictionary for weeks. *Epesu* has meanings such as to act, to treat, is, happens, to construct, to practice (as witchcraft), to sacrifice (as a bull). CAD wrestles ambiguities across 44 pages, and pins them to the mat with hundreds of citations and great flurries of definitions.

English may be rich, but it is short of equivalents for certain Akkadian expressions. Thus, English has a word for drawing the bow, but none specific to the act of shooting a bow. Akkadian does, and it provides words for the victims as well.

"*N* took us four months of checking, eight hours a day," said Dr. Gallery. "I lost five pounds."

"In my dreams I sometimes drop clay tablets and break them," said Dr. Hermann Hunger, a collaborator on CAD.

It would be difficult enough if Akkadian, a Semitic language, had been alone in Mesopotamia, but it co-existed with Sumerian, a language that belongs to no known family. Since Akkadian has many Sumerian loan-words, the CAD staff keeps a close watch on the work of Professor Miguel Civil, a colleague who is editing "Materials for the Sumerian Lexicon."

He treads warily. Take the Sumerian *naditu,* which seems to mean a woman dedicated to a god, usually unmarried, barred from having children, and living in a gagu. *Gagu* used to be translated as cloister, but now cautious scholars hesitate.

"What do you translate *gagu* as?" Professor Reiner asked Professor Civil recently.

"Gagu," he replied.

Since CAD is constantly beset by mysteries as it covers old ground, staffers are repeatedly tempted to write "mng. unknown" or "mng. uncertain." But that does not please Professor Reiner. "This is not a bland dictionary," she said. "We don't say only what's absolutely certain. We stick out our necks, and then somebody comes along ten years later and corrects the guess. I don't think corrections will come out unless we say something. One writes a dictionary *against* something—against an accepted opinion."

The University of Chicago has supported CAD these many years, and now the National Endowment for the Humanities is helping as well. So brisk is the demand that all the old volumes are being reprinted. The press run was originally 750, then it was raised to 1,000, 1,250 and now 1,500.

Akkadian's revival is plainly a matter of time. If the CAD staff seeks further consolation, Professor Reiner, whose linguistic legerdemain extends back to her native Budapest, offers it. "Hungarian is much more difficult," she said.

— — —

CHD, the *Chicago Hittite Dictionary*, will deal with the language recorded in cuneiform on clay tablets and spoken between 2000 and 1200 B.C. in what is now Turkey. Most of the tablets were excavated early this century, and they remained mysterious until Bedřich Hrozný, a Czech Assyriologist, made an inspired guess. In a sentence including the bread sign which he knew from Akkadian, he saw the words *ez-za-at-te-ni wa-a-tar-ma-e-ku-ut-te-ni*. *Ez-za* suggested the German "essen" (eat), and what was *wa-a-tar* but something to wash down the bread with? "So what he had with one stroke was that it was an Indo-European language," said Hans G. Guterbock, professor emeritus and co-director of the project.

From then on it was uphill sledding. In 1931 Edgar Sturtevant, a Yale professor, published a grammar and glossary, and finally Chicago and the National Endowment for the Humanities faced up to their responsibilities.

Professor Guterbock was an old hand at Hittite, having been on expeditions at Bogazkoy, first (1933–35) on a German dig, then on an American. His co-director, Professor Harry A. Hoffner Jr., describes himself as an armchair ttitologist. Both men compiled card files, and now CHD is being produced from half a million cards—about one-quarter as many as CAD boasts. About 30,000 clay tablets or fragments have been found, constituting about one-tenth the bulk of recovered Akkadian, or just enough to provide material for three dictionary volumes.

Historical texts abound—first-person royal reports and prayers, myths, epics, ritual guides and omen literature for untoward events such as eclipses and the birth of two-headed calves. Hittite enjoys a confusion of the species worthy of Sodom and Gemorrah. Storm god to mortal: "Ashertu is impugning thy virility. Although she is thy wife she keeps on sending to me: 'Come, sleep with me!' "

Occasionally, tablets are bilingual—Akkadian and Hittite—and thus easier to translate. "Sometimes we think there's a tablet demon," said Professor Hoffner, "because where there's Akkadian the Hittite is broken, and where Hittite appears the Akkadian is broken."

It can take 20 fragments to make a tablet. Not long ago, Professor Hoffner was working on a fragment that tapered off at the crucial juncture where the oracle tells how to punish the king's stepmother for using black magic to kill the queen. The oracle appeared to say that the gods forbade the king to slay his stepmother.

Dr. Howard Berman, who works on CHD, recalled seeing, in Professor Guterbock's collection, a transliteration of a word similar to one in the fragment. Examining that transliteration in the original Hittite, Professor Hoffner found that his fragment fitted perfectly onto Professor Guterbock's. Reconstituted, the text disclosed the godly worst: "Kill her if you want to."

Hittite has two genders, animate and inanimate (a dead

queen is animate for purposes of gender), and punctuation is reduced to a paragraph mark. Scholars have only vague notions about the sounds of Hittite, and pronounced difficulties with sibilants such as the one Professor Guterbock characterizes as "an s with air pressure behind it."

"I have dreamed answers to problems—once in a while correct answers," Professor Hoffner said.

"Once I dreamt that the B-volume had come out—beautifully illustrated," said Dr. Berman. "The first word was *babilili.*"

CHD will have no illustrations and there will be no B-volume. But there is a *babilili* (Babylonian), and for reasons that every Hittitologist can appreciate, it will be listed under *P.*

— — —

Room 216, home of the CDD, *Chicago Demotic Dictionary,* is never dusted, and the windows are never opened, for the slightest breeze could blow the papyrus fragments back into pre-Islamic chaos. Eugene Cruz-Uribe stands perplexed as he tries to fit fragments together. There are about 1,000 bits and pieces, and Mr. Cruz manages to place about one fragment a day.

The heat in 216 recalls that of Egypt, where Professor Janet H. Johnson, editor of CDD, is prospecting for additional scraps with which to try Mr. Cruz. "Once we get a papyrus put together we take a sentence, divide it into words, and make a card for each word," Mr. Cruz said. "With luck, we'll know what the word is."

Demotic, dominant in Egypt from about 650 B.C. to A.D. 450, succeeded hieratic, a cursive form of hieroglyphics. Hieroglyphs—pictographs—were deciphered thanks to the Rosetta Stone found by Napoleon's troops in 1799; the Rosetta Stone bore columns in hieroglyphic, Greek and demotic.

Demotic is known today from papyri and ostraca—broken bits of pot that have been scribbled on. In Athens, the name of a person to be ostracized was written on potsherd, but Egyptians would grab a pot even for routine declarations. Most of the discovered Egyptian pot-script has been published, but there are still about 2,000 bits of unpublished pot. Demotic also appears as graffiti on Egyptian monuments.

An awesome number of ostraca are legal documents complete with jargon, penalty clauses and fine print, making them almost as indecipherable as modern contracts. Many texts deal with tax evasion. Since Ptolemy kings held tax collectors personally responsible for tax collections, collectors vigorously pursued delinquents and the Ptolemys vigorously pursued tax collectors.

The University of Chicago caught up with demotic duties when a German scholar left his files, including dictionary notebooks, to a Chicago scholar who then worked sporadically on a dictionary. The Chicago scholar left his files to the Oriental Institute, which has the largest group of demoticists in the country.

George R. Hughes, demoticist par excellence and professor emeritus, has come out of retirement to teach demotic in Professor Johnson's absence, and to help with difficulties such as translations of the wisdom of Onchsheshonqy, the ancient Egyptian implicated in a regicide plot. Imprisoned, Onchsheshonqy called for papyrus but got pot from the vessels bearing his food and drink. On shards addressed to his son he wrote instructions such as "Inspect the house every hour that you may catch the burglar" and "Do not take liberties with a woman whose husband is listening to your words."

— — —

Professor Gene B. Gragg started out in cuneiform studies, dealt with pastimes such as Sumerian and Akkadian, and then decided to try living exotic tongues. After more than six years' work, the result is COD—*Chicago Oromo Dictionary;* the basic manuscript is complete.

Like most of Ethiopia's 70 languages, Oromo belongs to the Cushitic family, one of five families of the Afro-Asiatic group—the others are Semitic, Egyptian, Berber and Chadic. Professor Gragg is trying to learn something about the ancestral language of this group, which may have been spoken in the sixth millenium B.C.

In A.D. 1978, Oromo is spoken by about ten million of Ethiopia's 27 million people. Italian missionaries tried to transcribe it, but they were so shaken by the assault of Oromo's ten vowels, five short and five long, that they took refuge in familiar Italianate sounds.

Most of the time, Oromo has suffered in silence—a punishment decreed by Ethiopia's Amharic-speaking rulers. Pursuing a policy of national unification, Haile Selassie forbade the teaching of Oromo, but the new regime changed all that by deciding to promote literacy first and a national language second. The day Professor Gragg arrived in Addis Ababa, his quest financed by the National Science Foundation, broadcasting began in the liberated language. "I was able to take a complete bath in Oromo," Professor Gragg said.

Back in Chicago, he found Terfa Kumsa, an Oromo working his way through the University of Illinois, who welcomed extra money as a linguistic informant. "Tireless," Professor Gragg called him, noting: "In linguistic work, informants tend to tire after a half hour. They start looking for the door. But I'm the one who calls a halt—he'll insist he has three more words about the handle of a plow that I haven't got down."

Oromo has widely varying dialects and no recognized standard. In the East, for example, medicine is *d'awwaa*, and in the West *goricca*. The twain meet when speakers join the words in tandem, inserting *yookin* (or), and thus *d'awwaa yookin goricca*.

As he worked at COD, Professor Gragg kept finding old friends, such as Hansel and Gretel. Oromo's version is largely devoted to blood-curdling vengeance—the stepmother is impaled on sharp stakes in a hole and then boiling water is poured on her.

Before he was prepared to consider his own enterprise well done, Professor Gragg reviewed the work of Onesimus Nasib, an Oromo who was enslaved by the Sudanese and freed by missionaries who then sent him to school in Sweden. Onesimus found a way of writing in Oromo, and by consulting an Amharic translation put an entire Swedish Bible into Oromo. Gragg reviewed every word of the Pentateuch and New Testament.

With Marxism dominant in Ethiopia, there may be small demand for Onesimus's work—which was banned under Haile Selassie. But with Russians replacing the United States in Ethiopia, Professor Gragg expects the Soviet Union to be prime customers for his dictionary, COD.

French and English

René Ledésert and his wife Margaret (née Smith), spent a quarter of a century editing Harrap's New Standard French and English Dictionary, and they were still astonished at the confusion of species on both sides of the Channel. "*Le chat* (the cat) turned out to be in English different animals," he said, with the air of a Frenchman who has discovered that his favorite wine doesn't travel.

The French speak of buying a cat in the pocket; in English that is a pig in a poke. A cat in the throat in French is a frog in English. In French it is the long-suffering cat that turns, but in English it is the lowly worm. *Vache* (cow) is even harder to domesticate. A hungry man in France could eat a cow, but in England or America a horse. When the French say it's raining like a piddling cow, the English declare it's raining cats and dogs. The dictionary translates *être vache avec quelqu'un* (literally—to be cow with someone) as "to be a swine to someone."

Monsieur Ledésert and his English wife speak English to each other in England, French in France and muddy their palate with Franglais—which is neither here nor there—on the English Channel. Whichever way their lips move—whether with the transparent solidity of English or the liquid clarity of French—the words have a home at last in their new work.

The dictionary raised the bilingual standard right from the start, when Jean Edmond Mansion, the pre-war editor, moved to England and became John Edmund. René Ledésert stopped short of becoming Ronnie Desert, but he saluted bilingualism for a year at the University of Birmingham, and then pledged his allegiance by marrying Miss Smith, who was spending her year abroad at the University of Caen. After teaching French at Eton he applied for a job at Harrap's. "Do you collect stamps?" the company chairman asked him. When Monsieur Ledésert said yes, he was hired as just the right type to revise the firm's classic French and English dictionary.

Working at their 16th-century home in Holyport, England, with summers at their 17th-century home in Les Pilles, France, the Ledéserts—aided by Mrs. Ledésert's sister Muriel—made steady progress against the lexical accumulation of the centuries. When they disagreed on a word, Madam got final say on English and Monsieur had his way with French. The locutions of English still mark her French, the circumlocutions of French embroider his English.

"One thing is certain," he said. "Lately French has been borrowing more from English than English from French."

The first edition of the dictionary has held up remarkably in its French half. But, since English expressions dated more quickly, the English now has a distinctly Victorian pallor. Said Mrs. Ledésert: "When we include an obscene word, we mark it *V*—which stands for vulgar, really terribly vulgar. I also mark the really obscene words 'Not used in polite conversation,' and I write that very firmly. One doesn't want to be accused of not having rammed it home."

"English is much richer in obscenity," her husband said. In the new edition, Franglais appears, marked *F*—for familiar. "This is a dictionary for the user," Monsieur Le-désert said. "We're not bothering about the French Academy—it's 200 years behind the times."

The Academy works interminably to safeguard the French language by rejecting words it considers beneath the genius of French. Meanwhile, through subsidy to linguistic missionaries abroad and insistence on linguistic privilege in Europe, the French Government warns against alien forces who would confuse the case and despoil the gender.

Though France is of two minds about NATO, this dictionary enlisted the former head of NATO's translation service, and he betrayed bilateral usage secrets by the dozen. In this day of international friction, multinational corporations, common markets and Euro-crazes, a work like the dictionary is fundamental.

But some things probably will continue to move at the pace of an escargot. *"Insérer une pièce d'un franc dans la fente supérieure"* may forever remain "Insert a one-franc piece in the superior slot." And heaven forbid (an expression—*hélas!*—difficult to find in the new dictionary) that the French railroads give up their translation of *"Pour avoir de l'eau, tourner le robinet indifféremment à gauche ou à droite"*—"To obtain water turn the tap indifferently to the right or to the left."

The editors' English has a distinctly Anglo-Saxon tone, and Americans may find themselves up a gum tree (thrown for a loss) at (by) some of the equivalents. The new dictionary translates *A bas les vaches!* (literally—Down with the cows!) as "Shoot the bloody cops!" when the American version would more properly be "Kill the pigs!" In a proliferation of translations for the French *pipi*, the editors offer "to spend a penny" as well as "to shed a tear for Nelson."

An occasional mistake slipped past the proofreaders. For example, Napoléon, the Corsican corporal with little to lose, lost it. His accent disappeared. But the second printing restored the orthographic distinction, proving that you can lead a *corse* to Waterloo, but you can't make him shrink.

Estonian

Estonian has no articles, no gender, no prepositions, not much of a present and only a doubtful future. Ever since 1940, when the Soviet Union annexed the country to which 20 years earlier it had renounced all claims, Estonia has been struggling for its precarious identity and its forbidding language.

As heroes at home grapple with consonants innumerable, vowels almost interminable and Russian forever encroaching, Paul Saagpakk leads the fight abroad. Determined to save Estonian from native incomprehension and foreign assault, he has completed the epic work that could be the saving of the language—an Estonian-English dictionary.

"Poppa, you're crazy," his son would remonstrate. "You work 12, 14 hours a day and you won't get anything for it." Colleagues at the University of Massachusetts at Amherst, where Dr. Saagpakk teaches English literature, treated him as though he were mad. But the hours swept by, the days disappeared, and his only vacations were the hours of sleep each night; Dr. Saagpakk was sacrificing himself on the altar of patriotism, burying himself in the quicksand of synonymy.

"We have had a miserable history ever since the 13th century," Dr. Saagpakk said. "That's when the Teutonic knights brought Catholicism, and very roughly, with sword, blood and slavery. On my island of Saaremaa we were the last pagans, the Baltic Vikings. We've had the Germans, the Russians, the Poles and the Swedes—and now the Russians again. Three Britons sitting in the best hotel drinking fine whisky could colonize a whole country without attacking the local culture, but the Russians need three million people to control a country and they outlaw the local culture."

En route to his present indignation, Dr. Saagpakk attended five universities in five countries, and got his Columbia University doctorate with a thesis on psychopathological characters in English fiction. Sometimes he thinks of his own lexicography as a Dr. Jekyll-Mr. Hyde aberration. "You are caught by words and create your own world—like a schizophrenic. You struggle among words, you fight your troubles, and you emerge into paradise. I sometimes had to struggle for six hours to get the English equivalent of an Estonian term, but I like to struggle with difficulties and I won't give up. A dictionary man must have enormous endurance and patience, and without love you get nowhere. I have advised my students not to go into this work."

As word filtered from the Soviet Union of others struggling to keep their own language—Georgians, Armenians, Azerbaijanians—Dr. Saagpakk stepped up the pace. Estonian had already succumbed to Russian imports such as *kosmonavt, polkovnik* (colonel) and *agitprop* (propaganda agitation). Unaware of how odd it sounded to Estonians, Russians had even imposed *partorg* (party organizer), though in Estonian *part* means "duck" and *org* means "valley," making *partorg* the "valley of the ducks."

Relentlessly, Moscow pushed Russification of its northern colony, moving in Russians by the thousands, banning dissertations in Estonian and changing the very names on the map. A town like Kuresaare, metropolis of the island of Saaremaa, on which Dr. Saagpakk was born, suddenly became Kingisepp, in honor of the local communist martyr.

But it was the non-communist Estonians who felt like martyrs and saw the writing on the wall—in the Cyrillic of Russian instead of Estonian's own western alphabet.

Even in the best of times, Estonian is a minor child in the family of Finno-Ugric languages spoken by about 20 million people in the Carpathians and in the region between Norway and the Ob River in Siberia. Hungarian and Finnish are cousins, and there are other Finno-Ugric relatives that few have heard of and that virtually no one can speak, obscure languages such as Zyrian, Votyak, Olonets, Vepse, Lude, Cheremis and Vote. In these worst of times, the survival of Estonian seems doubtful.

Dr. Saagpakk embraced the battle in 1950, four years after arriving in America, when he realized that other refugees from his native country needed a reliable dictionary as much as he did, and that foreign students might want to learn Estonian. In 1959, desperately eager to concentrate on the dictionary, he quit a teaching job in New Jersey, borrowed $5,000 from a former student, and—like Noah Webster, who traveled to England—went abroad to improve his etymology. The American Council of Learned

Societies came to his rescue with grants, and by 1962 he had a manuscript. "Then I got so enthusiastic," he said, "that I started to enlarge and enlarge and enlarge."

Dismissing Russian loan words as "foreign vocables," he included popular Estonian terms familiar from his childhood. "Some people may be shocked," he suggested, "but I have used what I remember."

He offered the 9,000-page manuscript to the Yale University Press, and after a year Yale said yes. "They are slow but sure," Dr. Saagpakk said. "I don't blame them. Estonian is only one million people and practically unknown. And I'm very grateful to Yale for accepting, because it won't make any money."

For three years now, Yale and Dr. Saagpakk have been struggling to squeeze the manuscript into 1,200 printed pages. Estonian is such rocky soil that half the typesetting remains to be done, and Marian Ash, of the Yale University Press, has come to dread proposals for foreign-language dictionaries. "I try not to think about them before they come," she said.

But Estonians can hardly wait for publication. "This means a new era in Estonian," said Ilmar Mikiver, an Estonian author who works in this country.

"Estonian may one day be extinct, but my dictionary will survive," said Dr. Saagpakk, who continues to teach in the town that was formerly Noah Webster's home. "My classes are always doubled, although I am a damned foreigner. I started English at 12 years, and since then I have liked it, loved it, and still I haven't mastered it. Still I make mistakes and have an accent. My students are so polite they never tell me I have an accent, not in my good old U. of Mass."

In 1980, he will have to retire from the university, and his dream is to start then on an English-Estonian dictionary.

Ladino

When the inquisition drove them into exile at the end of the 15th century, many of Spain's Jews came as far east as Bulgaria, then ruled by the Turks. There, like their co-religionists who settled elsewhere in the Balkans or in the Mediterranean area, they spoke a language based on Ladino—a mixture of Catalan, biblical Hebrew, and Arabic borrowed from the Moors who invaded Spain.

Before World War II, there were 50,000 Jews in Bulgaria, but now there are only about 5,000, the vast majority of whom do not practice their religion. For years there has not been a wedding at the Sofia Synagogue, which has been in disrepair since bombardment in World War II; the congregation numbers only about twenty active members.

As assimilation increases many fear that their native, Ladino-based language will disappear. Today that vernacular is used mainly by the older generation, much as is the case elsewhere with Yiddish.

One of those in the older generation is Isaac Moscona, a retired shoe factory administrator who had agreed to be president of the Sofia Synagogue. Since his synagogue duties were undemanding, he did something about his fears for the future of his native language, spurred to action when he heard that the Ben-Zvi Institute at Jerusalem's Hebrew University was compiling a Ladino-Hebrew dictionary. On seeing specimen pages, he felt that Israeli scholars were going about the wrong job—producing a work for scientists, not people. He was concerned with the spoken language, not the original Ladino. So he got to work, and in three years completed a dictionary translating his Ladino vernacular— 16,000 words—into Bulgarian.

In his modest synagogue office, he traced the progress of his Ladino over the centuries. The lingua franca began with Catalan, to which the Jews of Spain added about 500 words of Hebrew, such as *rabbi* and *talis* (prayer shawl). From Arabic came words like *hazino* (sick) and *kira* (rent). Spanish Jews used the Arabic word for Sunday, since the Spanish *domingo* recalled *dominus*, which had a Christian sound to the Jewish ear. Spanish for *God* was *dios*, but the Jews used *dio*. *Dios* sounded plural, and the Jews daily affirmed in their prayers that God was one.

When the Jews fled from Spain to Bulgaria they found other Jews there whose own language had elements of Latin and Greek, the heritage of Roman and Byzantine domination. Since Spain's Jews had attained a high cultural level, it was their own language that eventually dominated in Bulgaria's community. It was nonetheless modified by local elements of Greek, Latin, and Turkish—Turkish alone contributed about 1,500 words.

More Jews came from Portugal, Hungary, Italy and Rumania. Those from Portugal contributed words like *akavidar* (warn) and *beso* (lip). From Italy came business terms such as *mostra* (sample), *commercio* (import duty), and

lavoro (work). By the 17th century the original Ladino had
become a modified tongue called Judeo-Spanish. It was of
course incomprehensible to the Ashkenazic Jews of Ger-
many, Eastern Europe and Russia, who spoke Judeo-
German, better known as Yiddish. During the 19th century
Jewish schools were implanted in the Mediterranean basin
by an association of French Jews. Since instruction was in
French, Judeo-Spanish incorporated a sizable element of
French.

It was this amalgam of influences which flowered by
the beginning of the 20th century that Mr. Moscona used to
compile his dictionary. Some of the words, such as *dias-
pora*, have an international ring, and despite differences
from country to country, this tongue is comprehensible
throughout the Mediterranean area.

Determined to preserve the linguistic richness, Mr.
Moscona included in his dictionary about 2,000 popular
expressions and proverbs:

"Aguas pasada no boltan mulino"—water that has
flowed by can't make the mill turn (don't cry over spilled
milk).

"Abasha eskalon, toma muzher; asuvi eskalon, toma
haver"—walk down a step and take a wife; go up a step and
take a partner.

"El paliko vino de ganedem"—the stick came from paradise. *Ganedem* is a direct borrowing from biblical
Hebrew.

The dictionary is neatly handwritten into two large
black volumes, and kept in the synagogue along with Mr.
Moscona's other work, such as his research on the surnames
of Bulgaria's Jews.

A member of the Bulgarian Academy of Sciences has

declared that Mr. Moscona's work should be published, lest the rich treasure constituted by this language be lost to posterity. But in communist Bulgaria, publishing is a state monopoly.

"If they tell me it can't be printed because sales would be too small," said Mr. Moscona, "or because the printing plan for the year is already fulfilled, I'll ask permission to export it to a foreign publisher. And if I hear nothing at all, I'll go to the mountain, just like Mohammed."

Six Thousand Dictionaries

Those who speak of looking up a word in the dictionary were not heartened by news that a publishing company was producing 6,000 different dictionaries.

Having decided to take the lexical world for its province, Books For Libraries, academic reprinters, began by scouring the secondhand book market for out-of-print works it wanted to reprint. It spent $750 for the six volumes of Robert Morrison's *Dictionary of the Chinese Language*, and 45 cents for a copy of D.N. Ushakov's *Orfograficheskii slovar* (Orthographic dictionary).

Soon the reprinted dictionaries began emerging in microfiche—96 or 98 pages miniaturized onto a 4×6 inch plastic card, for reading via a machine. One-tenth the list was also put out in hardcover.

Since Steven E. Hegaard, the project editor, is himself a Turkic scholar, as his Danish name would never indicate, Turkish dictionaries were the first available. Leading all the rest was *A Turkish and English Lexicon*, by Sir James W. Redhouse, orientalist in the British Foreign Office, and interpreter to the Grand Vizier. His dictionary came out in 1890, before Kemal Ataturk cut through the Arabic thicket and planted a variant of the Latin alphabet.

What a culture of scholars has trailblazed the forest of Altaic (Turkic, Mongolian, Manchu-Tungusic and Korean)! Russia's Nikolai Ivanobich Ashmarin (1870–1933), for example, took on Chuvash, and turned out a Chuvash-Russian dictionary in 17 volumes. Indiana University took on Ashmarin and began reprinting his work, only to run out of money after four volumes. Books For Libraries delivered Ashmarin from beginning to end.

Nikolai Alexandrovich Baskakov (born 1905) took Karakalpak (a dialect of Kazakh) for his very own—and produced the definitive work. At Columbia University, Mr. Hegaard found another Karakalpak expert in his own teacher, Karl Heinrich Menges, who had corresponded and exchanged visits with Dr. Baskakov. Professor Menges was earlier a fellow-student of the best-known Turkic expert, Gunnar Jarring, the Swede who served as United Nations mediator in the Middle East. In his youth, Dr. Jarring studied dialects of Chinese Turkestan and Afghanistan, and wrote about East Turki and Uzbek. Reviewing these studies, Professor Menges observed: "As [Dr. Jarring] proved to be an excellent field worker, it is particularly deplorable that he should have completely abandoned his work to enter the diplomatic service of his country."

For political—not scholarly—reasons, the Israeli government, which did not look kindly on Dr. Jarring's diplomatic accomplishments, might have seconded that notion. For scholarly—not political—reasons, the government nonetheless probably welcomed reprinting Dr. Jarring's book, *The Uzbek Dialect of Qilich*, and Israel's

officials surely acclaimed reprinting of the great *Dictionary of the Hebrew Language.*

This work by the neologizing lexicographer Eliezer Ben Yehuda took about 40 years of his life—and was a trial for his wife as well. She was terrified that a mouse might eat up her husband's notes. But he brushed aside her fears, explaining that a living Hebrew word is stronger than any animal.

The animal kingdom lurked menacingly also for other lexicographers. W.E. Soothill, who put together a popular Chinese-English dictionary, did wonders in conveying the sense of expressive Chinese characters such as the one he translated as "Bird of ill omen to State." Under "Cha (Dja)" he translated other characters with sequences suggestive of breakfast cereal: "twitter, whisper, answer;" "crack, clap, bang."

Dr. L. Wieger, a Jesuit who wrote *Chinese Characters* (one of the 6,000 works reprinted) took pains to illustrate how characters snap, crackle and pop. He traces the ideogram for *prince* through 45 centuries, explaining that it begins with: "A cap with horns, to inspire awe. Two arms, the executive power. A mouth, the legislative power." Many Mings later comes "a fanciful scribe who gave to the cap a curious form.... The next writer, an ignoramus, thought he saw two hands, instead of the horns on the cap.... An idle writer, for the sake of abbreviation, replaced one of the hands by a simple stroke..."

A Chinese dictionary by Herbert A. Giles points out that the Chinese didn't even have a term for grammar till foreign scholars filled the gap. He notes also that categories corresponding to our parts of speech, voice, mood, tense, person, case and number must be determined by context, usage, probability, inference and "general drift of the subject."

Dr. Giles cautions: "There is no noun-substantive in the Chinese language which might not, at the fiat of a master, be flung from his pen as a verb."

In *A Siamese-English Dictionary*, E.B. Michell warns that "common people constantly pronounce the letter *t* as a *k*, and not unfrequently pronounce the *k* as a *t*." (He takes a leaf from their book and notes that words beginning with one of the Siamese letters pronounced *s* will be found in his dictionary under *t*.)

Enter the Chinese. In Siam, Mr. Michell warns, they pronounce *r* as *l*—while others who would like to pronounce *r* as *l* have trouble getting the *l* out, and so, as he explains, "coolly omit the latter" (i.e. letter).

Conclusion? "No one will…suppose for a moment that the correct pronunciation of the Siamese language, with its infinitely varied modulations, can be learned by perusal of a dictionary."

Burmese is no simpler. Books For Libraries republished the *Burmese-English Dictionary* which was first bruited in 1913 and then took 27 years for the first installment. After ten more years came the second installment, along with an editorial note explaining: "The second world war gave the editors and printers preoccupations which interrupted the progress of the Dictionary."

"Death and other causes" removed most of the dictionary's correspondents. By the time Part V came out in 1968, all the dictionary's original sponsors had died.

The problems of the *Mongol-English Practical Dictionary* were with the living language rather than with dying sponsors. In the traditional Mongol written language, six vowels and four consonants are exactly like others.

Ambiguity is the curse of the struggling lexicographer. Captain James Kingston Tuckey, author of *Narrative of an Expedition to Explore the River Zaire, Usually Called the Congo, in South Africa, in 1816*—which provides one of the earliest Congo-English vocabularies—runs aground on one semantic sandbar after another. *White* is mistakenly translated as *bake*, *abroad* as *home*, *sunshine* as *shade*. Thanks possibly to the English habit of dropping h's, *mpou*—which means *hat*—is translated as *at*.

Doing its duty to scholarship, Books For Libraries was careful to publish also the more scholarly exploration of Congo vocabulary where it's hat.

Joys of Yiddish

When *The Joys of Yiddish* came out, its author, Leo Rosten, got a call from his mother. "You have saved Yiddish," she exulted. *"A leben oif dein keppeleh."*

Literally, Mr. Rosten's mother was saying to her son the author: "A life on your little head."

She should have wished his little head nine lives, because anybody who rescues Yiddish deserves the best—and occasionally gets just that. Mr. Rosten got the rewards of best-sellerdom and the trials of interviews, as in this *mish-mosh* (*hodge-podge*–p. 246).

"Yiddish is a Robin Hood," he said. "It steals—all right, let's say it borrows—from other languages. It borrows, it changes, it converts. And it gives to the rich, in other words, itself. Take words like *holdupnik* and *peacenik*. They come right from English, modeled on *nudnik*. Nobody knows where a *nudnik* (*pest*–p. 270) comes from, though everyone would like to send him back.

"In Israel you have an Academy that's forming new

Hebrew words. In Yiddish all it takes is English—*missiles, schmissiles.* What a rich language—so rich that there are no puns in Yiddish. How can you play on words when every word is playful?

"Since sacred discussion had to be in Hebrew, whatever was popular, playful, or frivolous was in Yiddish. Since Hebrew dealt with God, Yiddish turned to man and his earthly experiences. In poor lands, without radio or TV or movies, cut off from worldliness in literature, the Jew found escape in the embellishment of experiences.

"You know the story about the woman in the bus in Tel Aviv. Every time her son answered her in Hebrew she insisted he speak Yiddish. 'I don't want him to forget he's a Jew,' she explained."

As a dutiful son, Mr. Rosten has been helping others remember ever since 1935, when—aged 27—he created H*Y*M*A*N K*A*P*L*A*N, the immigrant who fractured English at his Americanization class.

A good many years later, Mr. Rosten began noting the extent to which English had borrowed from Yiddish. Then he saw an entry in *The Times Literary Supplement* that ran: "Should, schmould, shouldn't, schmouldn't." Before he could schmould regain his composure, he decided there was more to English—if only more Yiddish—than he had suspected. Where would we (or the English) be without such expressions as *kibitzer, meshugge,* and *mazel tov!* or simply *hoo-ha!, feh!, oy vay!,* and *ai-ai-ai!?*

"I saw how immensely expressive English had become thanks to Yiddish," Mr. Rosten said. "I think Yiddish has more nuances about personal characteristics than any other language I know. Take *nebach, schlemiel,* and *schmendrick.* Each has a special aroma and all mean so much more than "fool" or "misfit." You know what a *schlemiel* is, of course. He's a guy who buys a suit with two pairs of pants and promptly burns a hole in the jacket.

"In Yiddish I found an incredible richness of insight and aphorism. Take a saying like: 'The longest road in the world is the one that leads from the pocket.' or, 'When a father helps a son, both laugh; when a son helps a father, both cry.' It occurred to me there was a wonderful way to combine the parables and stories and words. I thought I should write a book of a hundred pages. So I formed a committee—including Orthodox, Conservative, and Reform rabbis—to help me."

The Joys of Yiddish spreads the pleasures across 533 pages. If Mr. Rosten had his way it would be used as a textbook. "I see no reason why you shouldn't get credit for Yiddish in high school or college—like any other language," he said. "If dead languages like Latin and Greek can earn credits, why should Yiddish be discriminated against? It isn't even dead. Must we wait for a decent burial before we take it seriously—or humorously?"

None of this is enough to placate Irving Howe, the critic, who complained that the jokes in the book were old enough to be eligible for a government pension. And many people consider Mr. Howe a *chachem* (*a savant, an expert, a brilliant mind, a man of learning and profundity*-p. 62), a chronicler of the intellectual scene from Kamenetz Podolsk (U.S.S.R.) to *Commentary* (A.J.C.).

What did Mr. Rosten think of Mr. Howe's scornful treatment? "He's entitled," Mr. Rosten said.

Anyone who thinks that reply is English had better think again. The absence of an indirect object after the adjective, and the inflection that—ideally—all but leaps from the printed page, qualify Mr. Rosten's oral shrug as the purest form of Yiddish.

Opting for a second opinion about Mr. Howe, Mr. Rosten declared: "A *chachem* he's not. He's a *mavin* (*a really knowledgeable person*–p. 223)."

He pursued: "Let Howe write 10 jokes and let me write 10 jokes, and you'll see the difference. When Freud wrote *Wit and the Unconscious*, nobody said, 'What a dull book.' People said, 'What insight to see such wit in the old stories.'"

But Mr. Howe will *krechtz* (*grunt-groan-croak-moan* or *wheeze*–p. 194) even louder when he hears the latest. Since Mr. Rosten has become a best-selling author, he was considering a sequel, to be called *The Added Joys of Yiddish*. It would include even more stories dear to his mother the *mameleh*, and old enough for his critic the *mavin*.

THE BRITISH

A British Concise
Dictionary Editor

A preliminary explanation is in order. What brings John B. Sykes to America? "The new edition of the *Concise Oxford Dictionary*—C.O.D.—is being published in the United States, and the editor—me—has come to America to talk to a few people and also to listen."

BRITISH English is what your dictionary is about, isn't it? "A dictionary has to be written in one English or another. We use an asterisk to denote American usage, and tram lines—parallel lines—for British usage."

CONCISE Oxford Dictionary differs in what ways from Shorter, Pocket, and just plain *Oxford English Dictionary?* "The 'plain' O.E.D. is of course the 12-volume affair which is now being augmented by four volumes of supplement. The Shorter is shorter than the O.E.D. but bigger than almost anything else. The Concise is shorter than the Shorter, but larger than the Pocket, and the Pocket is larger than the Little, which is reduced pretty much to definitions."

DICTIONARY buffs will find your work permissive, descriptive or prescriptive. Which shall it be? "We thought it best for the dictionary to represent English as it exists in public use, indicating cases where usage falls in the periphery of limited employ rather than in the central core of the language."

EDITOR of a dictionary was described by Samuel Johnson as "harmless drudge." Do you qualify? "Johnson described the lexicographer as a harmless drudge who busies himself in tracing the origin and detailing the significance of words. Is it drudgery? Sometimes."

FINDING the supply of words limitless, how did you decide what to include, what to omit? "A word like *eff-slicer* probably doesn't qualify for inclusion, but the meaning of *egghead* is by no means obvious from its constituent parts."

GOOD as an editor may be, how does he avoid moments of despair? "In the preface I quote from a predecessor: 'A dictionary-maker, unless he is a monster of omniscience, must deal with a great many matters of which he has no firsthand knowledge.' "

HUNTING through word lists is hardly what you expected to do with your life, is it? "After getting my doctorate in astrophysics and doing research in physics, I was a translator with the British Atomic Energy Authority. When the editor of the C.O.D. died in 1970, I got the job. But when I was young it never occurred to me that one had to sit down with slips of paper and actually construct dictionary entries."

IN what books and people did you find models for usage? "I tried to be aware of the usage at present in books, newspapers, magazines, all kinds of published English and spoken, too, and not only by those with considerable learning. Up to the fifth edition of the C.O.D., *trouser* as a garment, singular, is listed with the example, 'Here, again, is a smart & dressy trouser.' I imagine it came from one of the Fowler brothers, who edited the first C.O.D., visiting a tailor and noting down how the tailor spoke."

JUDICIOUSLY dealing with the riches of English requires what qualities? "What you need is not impatience, but resolution."

KNOWING that some words burst forth only to die, how did you decide which would survive? "Where you have a short history of a word, it is hard to decide. A transistor radio in Britain is often called *tranny*. I can see this is becoming established in Britain, but I didn't include it. Perhaps I made a wrong guess. There are 40,000 head words and not so many instances of that kind."

LEXICOGRAPHY has its pleasures. True or false? "Take the physicists' *quark*, one of three hypothetical components of elementary particles, which comes from Joyce's *Finnegans Wake*—'Three quarks for Muster Mark.' There's also pleasure in seeing how the language has developed from prehistoric roots such as the Germanic forms which are essentially reconstructions—words like *sun*, *star*, *night* and *day*. Other people, I'm sure, would find it deadly dull."

MUSES help the poet. Who helped you? "I don't even know that lexicography has a patron saint, though Johnson, Noah Webster and Sir James Murray are worthy candidates. Maybe they were chalcenterous—it means 'of brazen bowels'—able to carry on in the most incredible fashion for about 16 hours a day and to get it right at the same time."

NIGHTLY you devote yourself to crossword puzzles, don't you? "The London *Times* doesn't publish on Sunday, so I do the six they publish each week. The words are perfectly ordinary—it's the clues that are cryptic. *The Listener* puzzle is the most difficult in Britain. Sometimes they have circular puzzles or even mathematical puzzles in which the answers are numbers instead of words. The *Observer* has two puzzles—one fairly easy, the other more difficult. The difficult ones were started 40 years ago by an editor who used the pseudonym Torquemada—the Spanish Inquisitor. The current puzzle setter is Azed. That looks inoffensive, but when you turn it around it's the name of another Inquisitor. The chief crossword editor of *The Times* is named Akenhead, and that, too, seems appropriate in this context."

OVER the years, have you improved at solving puzzles? "I can do them much faster than when I started, 30 years ago. The puzzles in *The Times* take me about 10 minutes. This year I'm not participating in the national championship, since I won it four times in succession. The prizes are half a British gallon of whisky, and a fortnight for two in any European city with a Grand Metropolitan Hotel. In fact I didn't go anywhere, since I don't particularly like traveling abroad. So I gave friends the trip—one to Monte Carlo, two to Rome and one to Paris. I gave the whisky away, too, since I don't care for it."

PUZZLE questions must help you in dictionary work, or is it vice versa? "Dictionary work helps with puzzles, since it increases the vocabulary of words I can deploy."

QUESTIONS that puzzle others evidently pose fewer problems for you. How have you managed that? "One part of it is good fortune in identifying literary references. If you don't know the quotation only guesswork may help. One competitor in a regional final was faced with a Kipling quote, and he didn't know if it was *Gentiles* or *reptiles*. The quotation was 'Such boastings as the Gentiles use, Or lesser breeds without the Law.' He mentally tossed a coin and thought *reptiles* more akin to lesser breeds."

REVEALING yourself as a phenomenon of puzzles, can you describe your knack? "When I see a letter or two of a word—say the third and eighth letters—often the word will flash into my mind, whereas earlier I might have found the clue quite impenetrable."

SENSITIVITY to words is rare. Does puzzle-solving encourage it? "If people are solving puzzles with any thought, the interesting features of words can be useful. But if you're trying to be a champion solver, you often ignore the superficial meaning of the clue and thus miss some of the artistry—no time to savor the literal meaning let alone be deceived by it."

TO what lengths do you go in solving the puzzles? "Some puzzles offer prizes, and I just like winning things. *The Listener* has an annual dinner for its puzzle compilers, and this time they are inviting the solver who contributes the maximum number of correct solutions. When it's a matter of chance I'm not a lucky person. I never win the hamper of food in the church bazaar."

UNCOMMON words are often the most delightful. Have you given them their due? "We included *floccinaucini-hilipilification*, 'act or habit of estimating as worthless.' "

VERBALLY, people seem to be less skillful than formerly. True? "I rather have that feeling. I'm not sure it's a well-founded one."

WAYWARD citations, misleading clues, puzzles without end. How do you keep your balance? "By knowing that I don't have to do the puzzles unless I feel like it, and by trying to absorb all that might come in useful. In dictionary work, by realizing that language is multifarious and evidence infinite. The C.O.D. is a position statement, and I hope my position is balanced. Sometimes one finds that a definition is not right, after all. People write in and say, 'How could you?' One hopes to do better next time."

XENOGAMY, "cross-fertilization," is in C.O.D., but *xenogenesis*, "production of offspring permanently unlike the parent," is not. How did you decide to put one in and omit the other? "It can only be based on the evidence I have managed to gather that a word is rather widely used, or not requiring a disproportionate space for its inclusion."

YIELDING to the pressures of the age, you include common obscenities. Does that bother you? "The days of using a row of asterisks or an initial followed by a dash are gone, though over a wide range of publications there are corners where the decencies are still observed. But the words are frequently encountered, and when people meet this kind of word they're entitled to find it also in the dictionary and learn what it means. We use the label 'vulgar,' that is, 'to be used by those who have no wish to be thought polite or educated.'"

ZYMOSIS, "fermentation," is virtually the last word in your dictionary, and it aptly describes the language as well, doesn't it? "The language does constantly change, throwing up new forms, some of which are hardy and survive, while others sink back, disappearing into the fermenting mass."

A R Babcock

In the new *Concise Oxford Dictionary*, the editor's preface acknowledges the help of one rank outsider. "I would specially mention," as John B. Sykes puts it, "Mr. A.R. Babcock of Summit, New Jersey, the sender of frequent and interesting lists of suggestions since 1972."

Letters from Mr. Babcock arrive in a chaotic flurry, some by air, others by sea. All are by hand. "Not that I'm incapable of typewriting," he said, "but my mind keeps changing its ideas or its phraseology. Of course, I try to write as legibly as possible."

Dr. Sykes plainly has trouble keeping his head above the flurry. "I am very grateful for your continued flow of suggested improvements...," he wrote on May 14, 1973, and on April 9, 1976, to cover a period of less than three months: "Many thanks for a further 21 letters..."

Mr. Babcock was not easily discouraged, for he felt indebted to Oxford's lexicography. "Under the influence of H.W. Fowler, they have fostered the use of words in a stylistically effective and 'good' way," he said. "They have standards, which I find satisfying—a certain feeling that there's a right way of doing things, as opposed to a permissive or pragmatic way.

"There are two possible approaches to lexicography. The first is a scientific approach which tells how things are—what Merriam-Webster was criticized for in the third edition of its unabridged dictionary. There's a place for that—if you want to be a scientist. I should regret it if this purely objective approach wiped out the dictionary that suggests or hints at some preference."

But even dictionaries published by the Oxford University Press had apparent errors or omissions. Mr. Babcock started jotting down possible improvements and mailing them off. "In for a penny, in for a pound—it became an obsession with me," he said. Mr. Babcock is almost instinctively anglophile, his vocabulary a binational brew of English and American expressions.

At first, Dr. Sykes—a tall, ascetic-looking scholar—was unbending, and quick to offer objections: "The following seem to me to be too rare to justify inclusion: *analysis situs, clavier, eulogium, gillflert, grout* (= lees), *habitus, limbus, lupanar, protreptic.*"

Within just a few months, he had become warmly diplomatic: "I am very grateful for your continued flow of suggested improvements to the *Concise Oxford Dictionary*, and even if a few of the proposed additions prove to be already present the mere fact that they were not immediately obvious to a diligent reader such as yourself is a valuable indication that greater prominence is needed. For example, *formaldehyde* should not be concealed under *form-*."

"Your note on *voodoo*," he added, "is particularly helpful."

At the start, both correspondents were punctiliously

distant. Each addressed the other "Dear Sir," and the signatures were a coldly formal "A.R. Babcock" and "J.B. Sykes." With astonishing precipitation toward informality, the letter of Oct. 18, 1973 dropped "Dear Sir" in favor of "Dear Mr. Babcock," and Mr. Babcock reciprocated with "Dear Dr. Sykes." "Yours faithfully" became "Yours sincerely." In the letter from Oxford, dated Sept. 27, 1976, the signature is a boldly familiar "John Sykes."

Mr. Babcock had lots of time for considering the niceties of style, since he has spent his 58 years without benefit of career. "I've been pretty much of a failure in life," he said. "I've taught in schools briefly—English in Japan and in Guatamala. Sporadic, disconnected things. My independent income fostered my laziness, if that's the word for it."

His mother was French, his father a university professor of French. He was always interested in language and literature, beginning with Greek and Latin, extending to Icelandic and Sanskrit, and ending in an amateur's interest in English. When Dr. Sykes encouraged him, he began assiduous searches in the Summit public library, and took to discussing Dr. Sykes's letters with clerks in a local bookstore where his favor extends to little that is contemporary.

"Modern literature often concentrates on sexual abnormalities of all kinds, especially the more gruesome ones," he said. "I'm not a prude, but I prefer the old ways, the search for beauty. If there are certain laws and standards, there's more point in violating them. If there's no standard, there's the danger of everything becoming pointless."

He is equally impatient with a considerable run of popular usage: "Generally speaking, what upsets me is not so much single words or matters of pure grammar, but a tendency to use concealed clichés or figures of speech which through over-use are tiresome and could be shelved, for example *fallout* for 'result,' *surface* for 'appear.' It's a cheap way to try to make your prose vivid.

"There are hierarchies of clichés, from the unspeakable—I'm afraid they get spoken—to others one can hardly avoid, for example 'better late than never.' I especially dislike 'moment of truth.' In the Spanish bullring—I abhor bullfighting—it has its place. Will the bullfighter move a fraction of an inch or stand his ground—that is a moment of truth. But when you use 'moment of truth' for whether it's raining, that's obnoxious."

"I'm very often at a loss for words," he noted, and so saying he drew from his pocket a well-worn wallet, which he called a *purse*, and displayed slips of paper for noting new usages. "I attach these what-do-you-call-thems with these whats-the-word." The word was *paper clips*.

As the intelligence from the slips made its way to Oxford, Dr. Sykes became increasingly curious about his altruistic correspondent. In mid-1974 he wrote that he imagined Summit "as being at the top of a conical hill." Mr. Babcock replied that there were hills around, but he didn't know which one had given rise to the name.

"Since this is voluntary work, and I can follow my own rules," he suggested, "I've taken the liberty at times of being facetious, and I try to use what sense of humor I have."

Thus, he objected to the definition, in the previous edition of the C.O.D., of *courtesan* as "prostitute." "That's like defining a palace as a house, or a cardinal as a priest," he said. In the new edition, *courtesan* has accordingly been expanded and elevated to "prostitute, esp. one whose clients are wealthy or upper-class."

When Dr. Sykes visited America in 1976, the two men

met at a party in honor of the editor. Then Dr. Sykes returned to his domestic heath, and Mr. Babcock to his local prominence. Since then, the New Jersey benefactor has been poring over the latest C.O.D. for signs of the effect, not to say fallout, of his assistance. "With such a vast improvement in the new edition, thanks to Dr. Sykes, I imagine it'll mean there will be a good deal less to help him with," he suggested.

That conclusion seems premature or at least theoretical, to judge by Dr. Sykes's most recent missive, which begins: "First let me say what a great pleasure it was to meet you in New York and discuss various topics of mutual interest. Since returning, I have had many letters from you..."

Oxford English Dictionary

The harmless drudges who had spent fifteen years preparing a supplement to *The Oxford English Dictionary*—that monument to the arbitrary splendor of the English tongue—were finally ready to declare a 1,356-page dividend.

Oxford's heirs to Samuel Johnson, author of the first great English dictionary—it was he who defined lexicographer as "a harmless drudge"—had written the last word in the first volume of four which will constitute the supplement. When Volume I finally came out, it covered English language development from 1884 to the present, from *A* to *G*. Volume II quickly followed, from *H* to *N*.

A to *Z* in the original 15,487 pages of the O.E.D. emerged in the years 1884 to 1928, and a first supplement followed in 1933. Oxford then slumbered while English leaped on.

In 1957 the Oxford lords of language decided to catch hold again, and recruited Robert W. Burchfield as editor. Mr. Burchfield had come to Oxford as a Rhodes scholar in 1949 from his native New Zealand. He had become a specialist in medieval English, and he still teaches it at St. Peter's College. He knew little about lexicography, but he knew Charles T. Onions, one of the four editors of the original O.E.D., and one of the two editors of the 1933 Supplement.

"Onions said that lexicography is best done on the kitchen table," Mr. Burchfield said. "He didn't believe in computer techniques, photostats, typewriters. The only way to do it was to get people to read books, scientific journals and newspapers—build up the scientific evidence and then settle the dictionary on their backsides at the kitchen table.

"He also argued strongly that you should never submit to a deadline. But a historical dictionary always takes about 20 times as long as the normal one. People are born, get married and die before the dictionary gets out. The right policy is to do the things you can without holding up your dictionary for years and without killing off your staff. There are people who want you to pause for a year while a field worker goes out to determine who says *genuine* (rhymes with "gin") and who says *genuine* (rhymes with "wine"). There are no natural limits to words. The O.E.D. took forty-four years to complete; if you want to give more and more information you may be led up the garden path."

Mr. Burchfield's colloquial preferences are by now almost inextricably polycentric. If he says "up the garden path" on one occasion, he is just as likely to say "up a gum tree" on the next. Notable in his speech are the idioms of New Zealand. "I should think there's a high percentage of New Zealand English in the Supplement," he acknowledged, "but people in Oxford are putting gentle restraints on me."

There is nonetheless a fine cover of alien mulch. As Mr.

Burchfield notes in the Supplement's Introduction: "We have made bold forays into the written English of regions outside the British Isles...."

Campaign headquarters is in the Jericho section of Oxford, at 40 Walton Crescent, in a house that would be considered nondescript by anyone less richly endowed in verbal resources than its occupants. Mr. Burchfield calls it "a Victorian nightmare."

A historical dictionary lives or dies by its quotations, and Oxford's are divided between the top and bottom of the nightmare. In a large cupboard at the top is the legacy of crumbs from Mr. Onions's kitchen table. "No set size of slip—in rubber bands or string," Mr. Burchfield noted. "The old boys loved the backs of envelopes. We've had nothing but six-by-four-inch slips since I arrived. That's the climactic change I introduced."

Post-1957 standardized slips are ranked in filing cabinets at the bottom of the house—almost two million citations.

"The O.E.D. virtually concordanced the early writers—Chaucer, Malory, Langland, and just about every singular occurrence of a word is in the dictionary," Mr. Burchfield said. "If you move to the twentieth century you can't put in every word that Robert Graves, W.H. Auden, Stephen Spender, and W.B. Yeats have used. We've fallen back on the technique of generous representation. If we included everything it wouldn't be better, it wouldn't be more useful, because it would never get done."

His staff tried to determine which would be central and enduring terms in the newer disciplines. "You've got to be a bit of a forecaster," Mr. Burchfield said. "Take linguistics. Chomsky came up like a comet, and his subject has produced a whole group of words—we have generative **grammar**, transformational grammar, kernel sentences, **rewrite** rules, tree diagrams."

Modern linguistics is what Mr. Burchfield might term his *bête noire* (an expression listed in the Supplement). "The transformational grammarians tend to fasten on one word and give it hell," he complained, "not seeing that there are 414,000 head words in the O.E.D. When I was in New York for a lexicographers' conference, one professor gave a whole paper on the words *know* and *believe*. Dictionaries do disambiguate these two constructions if only the transformational grammarians would take the trouble to consult big dictionaries instead of small ones."

Mr. Burchfield's use of the word *disambiguate* raised four eyebrows—those belonging to Sandra Raphael and to Alan M. Hughes, of the Supplement staff. "Scientific jargon," Mr. Burchfield apologized. "Scientific jargon is superior slang," Miss Raphael suggested, smiling.

She is the specialist on plant and animal terms, and Mr. Hughes does hard sciences. They share an office and occasionally collaborate on a word such as *cannabis*. Miss Raphael explained: "I did the botany and Alan did the chemistry, and the social consequences fell into place on their own."

This chemical compound takes almost a column of tight print, highlighted with references to Greek and Latin as well as eighteenth-, nineteenth-, and twentieth-century sources—and finally an unabashedly provincial quotation from the Oxford *Mail* of April 8, 1970.

To get to the roots of *cannabis*, the staff sent queries to the Oxford University Press branch in Bombay, and to Washington, where one O.E.D. employee works full time at the Library of Congress. Another staffer works at the British Museum, and yet another at the Colindale Newspaper Reference Library, which gets a copy of every daily newspaper in Britain.

"Knowing where to look is not really a problem," Mr. Hughes said. "There are two main problems. One is finding the first use of a term, and the other is finding out precisely what a term means. *Gene* was very difficult, and I'm not entirely satisfied with the definition we wound up with in the Supplement. Now it's more a biochemical than a biological notion."

> gene: Each of the units of heredity which (except for polygenes) may be regarded as the controlling agents in the expression of single phenotypic characters and are usu. segments of a chromosome at fixed positions relative to each other; they were orig. defined as ultimate units of mutation and recombination, but are now best regarded as sequences of nucleotides within nucleic acid molecules each of which determines the primary structure of some protein or polypeptide molecule.

"The people who did the original Dictionary, and the original Supplement, were arts people who gave grudging consent to science," Miss Raphael noted. "There are a lot of plants going into the Supplement that I should have expected to find in 1933."

On the Supplement staff are a score of specialists. "Twenty sophisticated people's time is all I can organize," Mr. Burchfield said, "or twenty people's sophisticated time."

The sophisticated Anthony J. Augarde was at Oxford reading English when his tutor—Mr. Burchfield—recruited him to the cause. "One of the joys is that you're doing encyclopedic reading in almost every subject, hopping from one to another," Mr. Augarde said. "In theory you should end up with encyclopedic knowledge. In practice you don't. A word I've worked on will ring a bell if I hear it again, but I probably won't remember what it means—so this isn't a way to improve your vocabulary.

"I hate Scrabble, because it's a game lexicographers ought to be able to play and I'm hopeless at it. All the words I know are over seven letters."

Mr. Augarde spent three months on the entries for *go*, which go on for three pages. He also did *get* and *give*, each of which gets another three pages, give or take a column. Poaching on scientific preserves he cheerfully admitted that *ecodoom* and *ecodoomster* hit the language too late for inclusion. "Words like *megadeath* seem passé," he observed happily.

Mr. Burchfield appeared less emotionally involved. "Every single word is interesting," he said. But even he admitted that some words are more interestingly complicated. "*Anti-* is one of the most prolific forming-elements in the twentieth century," he noted. "*Air-* and all its formations caused us to be delayed for quite some time."

"There is an interesting group of words that you can spell any way you feel like," he went on. The Supplement warms up to this exercise with a paroxysm approximating the common sneeze: *atishoo, atichoo, atcha, a-tschoo, a-tischoo, er-tchiou.*

By page 796 the Supplement is daringly replete with multiple decisiveness. *Didicoi* there is equally acceptable as *didicoy*, either denoting a *gipsy* (or even a *gypsy*). But variants accumulate: *didakai, didakei, diddekai, diddicoy, didekei, dideki, didekie, dideky, didikai, didikoi* and *didycoy*. *Diederik* (an African cuckoo) is equally distinguishable and acceptable as *diedrik*, and hardly less admissible as *didric* and *diedrick*. *Diddy* (breast or nipple) is barely camouflaged as *deddy* and *diddey*. *Didgeridoo* (a musical instrument of Australian Aborigines) sounds as sweet spelled *didjeridoo*, *didjeridu* and *dijiridu*. *Didy* (U.S. colloquial for *diaper*) is also done up as *didie*.

When work began in 1957, no general English dictionary contained what Mr. Burchfield calls "the more notorious of the sexual words," but—as he proclaims, resorting to French for his sexual resolution: *"Nous avons changé tout cela."*

The Supplement leaves the Victorian O.E.D. firmly behind and catalogues current usages, including the common copulative (first citation about 1503). The governing entry reads: "For centuries, and still by the great majority, regarded as a taboo word; until recent times not often recorded in print, but frequent in coarse speech."

Surveying the vast resources of the past was the awesome duty of a free-lance staff of academics from all over Britain who agreed to read within the period 1884 to the present. About a hundred readers were finally at work, each getting seven shillings and sixpence (then roughly a dollar) an hour. "It was pretty rough justice," Mr. Burchfield said, "because some produced extremely valuable stuff and some produced almost nothing."

The oldest reader was Rev. H.E.G. Rope, a cleric in his nineties, whose name is on the list of those who contributed to the O.E.D. itself. R.A. Auty, a retired schoolmaster, was the most prolific paid reader—he went through 900 books, including most of T.S. Eliot, D.H. Lawrence, and James Joyce, and also *The Times* 1958–67, *The Times Literary Supplement* 1930–38, and thickets of linguistics, cricket, and bridge.

"In the Isle of Wight prison," Mr. Burchfield said, "a Cambridge student (he seemed to put ever so slight an emphasis on *Cambridge*) being held for a drugs offense asked for permission to compile a collection of current British prison slang for the O.E.D. He got permission."

Mr. Burchfield printed appeals for help that were slipped into copies of *The Periodical*, a quarterly giveaway from the Oxford University Press. The first appeal, in 1958, was a seven-page list of words beginning with *A* (road class) and ending with *akka* (slang, piastre). Beside each word was a date indicating the earliest use discovered. By 1961 Mr. Burchfield's appeals reached their last word—*zwitterionic* (*zwitterion* is "a molecule or ion that has separate positively and negatively charged groups; a dipolar ion"). Readers were challenged to document uses earlier than those cited.

"It produced an enormous response," Mr. Burchfield recalled. "Those who wrote in absolutely demolished the original dates."

The most significant response came from Marghanita Laski, an enormously erudite book reviewer, who volunteered her services free. What set her off was the date 1946 beside the term *alley cat*. Miss Laski recalled Don Marquis's alley cat, mehitabel, vintage 1927, and she requested slips to list such findings. She was sent a dozen.

Alley cat was subsequently traced to Ezra Pound and 1914, and Miss Laski was eventually fitted out with more and more slips. In the end she furnished over 100,000 citations, having read—or reread—George Bernard Shaw, Max Beerbohm, Ernest Hemingway, Louis MacNeice, Elizabeth Bowen, Graham Greene, Ogden Nash, and John Osborne. She also took on fashion, food, social life in general, sewing, embroidery, gardening, and what the English call *cookery.* (Nodding at the controls, Mr. Burchfield listed this ultimate Laski specialty in his Introduction as *cooking.*)

Miss Laski apparently never nodded. Since she is a quick reader she also devoured *The Guardian* and *Encounter. The Guardian* was a fine source, she reported later in an absorbing account in *The Times Literary Supplement*, except that many of the apparently new terms turned out to be misprints. *Encounter* she abandoned, deciding that too many of its words began with *anti-.*

To keep herself in positive-thinking periodicals, she substituted *The Listener*, organ of the B.B.C.—which is familiarly known in Britain as Auntie. Miss Laski ignored the coincidence.

In addition to providing numerous antedatings, she furnished postdatings as well—the continuing use of words that the Oxford staff thought obsolete. On occasion she even slipped such words into articles she wrote for *The Guardian*, then mailed in slips citing her own use. Her principal problem was remembering the order of letters in the alphabet, particularly the sequences from H to K, O to Q, and U to Y.

For all these weaknesses that the flashy Miss Laski was heiress to, she was regarded with undiluted awe in Oxford. An example was the tribute paid by John Sykes, editor of *The Concise Oxford Dictionary.* "None of us would dream of reading *The Guardian* after Marghanita reads it," he said.

The combined staffs of all Oxford dictionaries gather each afternoon for a leisurely cup of tea and an extended exchange of words. They have preserved many of the kitchen-table methods of Mr. Onions, for example, abhorrence of typewriters. All slips prepared by the staff, and virtually all citations turned in by readers, are handwritten, as is all material submitted to the printers. "I recognize the signatures of all the readers," Mr. Burchfield said. "You never forget a handwriting once you've dealt with it. The only ones that fox me are the slips that are typed. The only person here who types is my secretary, and she works only in the morning."

"Her typewriter is in poor repair," Mr. Augarde said, "and there are evil noises coming from it."

"I have the greatest admiration for the Merriam-Webster people in America," Mr. Burchfield went on. "They have more typists than we have editorial staff. My own view is that the collection at Springfield—they have about twelve million quotations—and our own here keep the English language in order."

The Supplement cites authors and speakers beginning with King Alfred (849-99). "On every page you'll find evidence of James Joyce and Kipling and H.G. Wells," Mr. Burchfield said. "There are generous references to Yeats, Auden, Eliot, Dylan Thomas, Nabokov, Spock. We call them 'significant authors.' Wodehouse is just as fruitful a source in the 1970s as he was in the 1920s. D.H. Lawrence is as frequent as Wodehouse."

Adlai Stevenson gets credit for *brinkmanship* and *egghead*, Eisenhower for applying the *domino* to strategy (his phrase in 1954 was *the "falling domino" principle*). Queen Elizabeth II is cited under *butterflies*, having spoken of the kind that flutter in the royal stomach. Her *corgis* are given firm leash on enduring life in the Supplement, which cites a caption in *The Times* (1970): "The Queen, with a firm hand on the leash for a reluctant corgi, arriving at Euston station." The Oxford specialists have kept a firm hand on the whole entry: they list *corgy* as well as *corgi*, and note that the plural of this originally Welsh word is not only *corgis* but *corgwn.*

Theodore Roosevelt carries a big stick of type on *big-game hunting.* Herman Kahn introduces a bigger threat under *escalation.* Henry A. Kissinger is cited from his *Problems of National Strategy,* and Herman Clarence Nixon from *Forty Acres and Steel Mules.*

The final volume will include a list of the 40,000 books cited. Michael Grose, the Supplement's bibliographer, calls this "adding the veneer of bibliographic respectability."

"I think the British Museum is eight times as large as it was 100 years ago, and if anyone's to find the books we quote from we have to give more information than the O.E.D. gave," Mr. Burchfield said. "Obviously, in the case of the Smiths, the Joneses, the Robinsons, we have to give all the initials they bear. We have to be equally generous in reference to periodicals. So many published reports are called *English Studies.* You can't just put *Eng. Stud.* and hope for the best.

"When we quote Nancy Mitford's *Pigeon Pie* we quote it always 'N. Mitford *Pigeon Pie,*' not 'Mitford, N. Pig. Pie.'"

The letter A is not as up-to-date as the letter G, since it went to the printer earlier. The first full word after numerous entries for various uses of *A* and *a* is *aa.* "I never attempt to pronounce it," Mr. Burchfield said. "It's a Polynesian word which means a kind of lava."

Biafran just managed to get in, though the country is now out. *Anguillan, Chicano* and *downer* (a drug which depresses or sedates, also a depressing experience) missed the deadlines.

"I ended the first volume at *G,*" Mr. Burchfield said, "and my science editor didn't agree it was the right place, didn't like my homely method, because he was doing a probability theory."

The second volume emerged in 1976, and the third was to follow a mere two years later. "Sometimes that sounds fantastically ambitious," Mr. Burchfield said. "We'll have to put our heads down again very hard, to get a good installment in the press. That's when it becomes more like a military operation than a scholarly one."

Unless some zany neologism appears, the final volume will conclude with an appropriately ultime *zzz*. Anyone who gets that far will deserve his rest.

Oxford Dictionary of English Proverbs

The *Oxford Dictionary of English Proverbs* begins: "Wise men make proverbs and fools repeat them."

The book then ignores this ancient wisdom and proceeds—in 930 pages—to a refreshed inventory of the sages.

It had been twenty-two years since the second edition of this compilation of pithy summaries of popular wisdom, and the new work was the result of the late Professor F.P. Wilson's lifelong interest in proverbs. He approvingly quoted the words of an eighteenth-century predecessor who maintained that he pursued the work "without any Regard either to Honour or Profit, but only to give myself a Harmless, Innocent, Scholar-like Divertisement in my declining years."

Francis Bacon once said the "genius, wit, and spirit of a nation are discovered by their proverbs," but if this is so it takes only a cursory shuffling of pages to discover that English nation speaks with forked tongue.

"Boys will be boys," goes one proverb. "Boys will be men," assures another.

"The face is the index of the heart," maintains an ancient proverb. "The face is no index to the heart," goes another proverb, and Shakespeare gave that one voice in *Twelfth Night.*

If proverbs straddle the fence of wisdom, now urging a stitch in time, now recommending a look before one leaps, they merely illustrate the proverb that "Every medal has its reverse."

Occasionally proverbs swell from pitch to full-bodied poetic expression. Shakespeare took "Make hay while the sun shines" and made it:

"The sun shines hot, and if we use delay,
. Cold biting winter mars our ho'd-for hay."

Chaucer was forever expanding proverbs, and sometimes he, too, seemed to be paid by the word. "Mum's the word," that is, "Silence is golden," became for him: "These wyse clerkes then ben dede Han ever yet proverbed to us yonge, That 'firste vertu is to kepe tonge.'"

America's foremost practitioner of the art was Benjamin Franklin, and he, too, plundered earlier wisdoms. "Time is money," he said, as had the Greeks and also Bacon.

Many proverbs with modern ring have ancient source. "Kill two birds with one stone"? Ovid wrote: *"Unus cum gemino calculus hoste perit."* Other versions of this elementary strategy abound: "To kill two flies with one slap." "To stop two gaps with one bush." "To stop two mouths with one morsel."

"He has more guts than brains" was in a 1678 collection.

"Corporations have neither souls to be saved nor bodies to be kicked" comes not from John Kenneth Galbraith but from an eighteenth-century Lord Chancellor.

The wisdom of the proverb can be used to damn as well

as praise, and lawyers may consider suing the publisher to correct their image: "In a thousand pounds of law, there's not an ounce of love." "One law for the rich and another for the poor." "Law is a bottomless pit" (also a cormorant and a harpy). "Law, logic, and the Switzers fight for anybody."

The book treads firmly in the realms of old, dutifully presenting original versions of many proverbs tidied by time, leaving a reader free to choose among the riches. A simple concept like love, for example, is said to be a sweet torment, bitter-sweet, blind, never foul, free, full of fear (or trouble), lawless, the fruit of idleness, and without reason. One can easily be intoxicated with love, or merely drunk as a beggar, fiddler, lord, mouse, rat, wheelbarrow, Chloe, or David's sow.

Sad to report, the century's premier paroemiologist—Nikita S. Khrushchev—is an offstage voice in this collection, for his proverbial wisdom is not yet taken as English. By the fourth edition, the dictionary may make honorable amends.

It was Khrushchev who said, "The dog barks and the wind carries it away." (In the dictionary, an anonymous old Moor is given credit for an earlier version: "Dogs bark, but the caravan goes on.")

"You may call me a pot, but don't put me on a stove," said the leader of all the Russians before he was called even worse and put on ice.

The Russians have long maintained that you can't get away from a proverb, and their cousins in Kirghizia have even higher praise. A proverb there proclaims that just as the beauty of the chin is the beard, the beauty of speech is the proverb.

THE AMERICANS

Webster's New Collegiate Dictionary

Dr. Henry Bosley Woolf was editor in charge of dictionaries for the G. & C. Merriam Company in Springfield, Massachusetts, and his preferences as to correct usage were pronounced. "I would never use the word 'finalize,'" he said. "And I shudder when I hear people say forMIdable and harASS."

He nonetheless banned the word "correct" from the office. "We use the word 'acceptable,'" he explained. "The average person thinks there's one way of pronouncing a word, and it simply isn't the case. There's more than one way of going from here to New York, and there's more than one way of pronouncing words. A dictionary has got to indicate the variety. You put one word ahead of the other simply because you can't print one on top of the other.

"In this country there are too many people who speak the several leading dialects, and none has preeminence over the others," said Edward Artin. He was Merriam's expert on orthoepy, which means pronunciation—though there's no agreement on how to pronounce *that* word, either. Submerged under tape recorders and radios, he harked to the unguarded syllable for earsay evidence.

At Merriam, huge files record the varying pronunciations for individual words. A sterling example is *economics*. Whenever Mr. Artin computed preference the result was about 50 percent for the first syllable rhyming with peck, 50 percent for rhyming with peek. George S. McGovern and Nelson Rockefeller were in the pecking order, but not Kingman Brewster Jr. or Arthur J. Goldberg. *Ecological* is similarly divisive, with Barry Commoner pronouncing it eecological and Lewis Mumford eckological. *Divisive* itself is divisive, with the second *i* as in "die" or as in "dill." President Johnson divided his favor between the two versions, but President Nixon never said vie.

"Roosevelt was about the best American public speaker I ever heard," Mr. Artin said. "Adlai Stevenson was excellent, though he pronounced *elite* 'eelite' and said 'surveyance' for *surveillance*."

Mr. Artin liked to think he had become liberal about pronunciation, but he abhorred the failure to distinguish between *finger* and *singer*, and the insularity of those who said "Lungisland." "Most Americans make no distinction in pronunciation of *latter* and *ladder*," he noted. "And it amazes me to hear an English 'banahna.' I break down laughing."

Queen Elizabeth II speaks of "ALlies." So does W. Averell Harriman, who was Ambassador to Her Majesty's Government, but Mrs. J. Borden Harriman, his cousin by marriage, who was U.S. Minister to Norway, calls them "alLIES."

It pleased a professional like Mr. Artin to track amateur's status. Truman Capote and Bing Crosby pronounced it "amater." "Amature" or "amatour" was the favorite of Robert M. Hutchins and Alfred Gruenther. Ethel Merman called it "amachur," as did the two Jacks (Benny and Paar) and the one Phil (Silvers). Howard K. Smith wobbled between "amater" and "amature," and Eric Sevareid between "amatour" and "amachur."

In *Webster's New International Dictionary Second Edition* (the Merriam unabridged which came out in 1934), the pronunciation of *Algonquin* was given as "Algonkin," but Mr. Artin learned better. His file revealed that Frank Case, former manager of the Algonquin Hotel in New York, pronounced it "Algonkwin." Andrew A. Anspach, a subsequent manager, said that even the Algonquin Indians knew that was right.

William A. Llewellyn, executive vice-president of Merriam, had the greatest sympathy for orthoepic dilemmas. He noted that even *ecumenism,* so favorable to tolerance, had two sides: "The President of Notre Dame says one thing, and the President of Boston College says another." (Right in the dictionary office some people pronounce the company name "Miriam.")

Like monks at their daily devotions, the dictionary staff was expected to spend an hour each day reading and marking books, newspapers and magazines, and there were over 12 million word citations in the files.

In the New Collegiate the late Bishop James A. Pike was cited for his *risibility* ("our risibilities support us as we skim over the surface of a deep issue"). Max Beerbohm, who wrote a story about a man returning to life and checking his fame in the catalog of the British Museum, was here immortalized for the single word *as* ("his face was as a mask").

And who knew more than Ezra Pound about *do's* and *don'ts,* as in his phrase cited here ("there are simply certain things he don't know")? Albert Shanker was remembered for *excess* ("we need a stronger central board to prevent excesses and abuses by newly created local powers"). Casey Stengel, long celebrated for innovative prose, was memorialized here for *glove* ("he's got a good glove at three positions and can pinch-hit").

Dr. Woolf was reluctant to cite anything from prepared texts by modern Presidents or by Cabinet members, since these were almost certain to be ghostwritten. Spiro Agnew was nowhere cited but Nixon was allowed to illustrate *netherworld* ("the netherworld of deceit, subversion, and espionage").

Some of the Merriam editors had doubts about the qualification "popular usage," but not Mairé Weir Kay. She wrote the files a pink slip declaring that the term "is not meant to be derogatory; it means the way language is used for normal human purposes, not trammeled by pedantry nor etiolated by literary cultivation."

For all kinds of purposes the language had been growing so quickly that Merriam had to scurry to keep up with mutants in fields such as sports, computer science, the drug subculture, molecular biology, immunology, genetics, neurosciences and ecology.

Roger W. Pease Jr., a butterfly biologist, was the editor specializing in science terms, and numerical taxonomy (which accumulates butterfly measurements) gave him lots of new concepts to light on.

His heart leaped up when he beheld the word *introgeneous* three times in Thomas H. Huxley's *On the Origin of Species*, as when Dr. Huxley traced the horse back to "a minute particle of introgeneous matter." Eventually Dr. Pease discovered it was a typographical error for *nitrogeneous*.

Dr. F. Stuart Crawford, who was in charge of Merriam's etymology, was alert to the errors of origin. "We get a lot of letters from people saying a word comes from Yiddish," he said. "Then we look for the word in Yiddish and can't find it."

He was weary of rejecting the popular belief about mysterious *posh*. It is not an acronym of the expression "Port Out, Starboard Home." Dr. Crawford was still prospecting for the sources of *nitty gritty* and of *gazump*, and he asked, "Why should marijuana be called pot?"

Candidates for the next dictionary were James G. Lowe's province, and he was scrutinizing neologisms such as *logophag* (one who eats one's words—Stewart Alsop's term for George McGovern), *tenuree* (one who is tenured), *kissee* (one who is kissed), *uncorpse* (one who is).

"We try to have a range of sources and about a five-year spread for a word to make sure it isn't ephemeral," Mr. Lowe said. "Some words, such as *sputnik*, are important as soon as they're used. The importance of other words doesn't become evident until long after their first use. The first citation for *atomic bomb* we have is 1917, but it wasn't put in a dictionary until 1947."

At Merriam the assumption was that the Collegiate would go on forever. So may the unabridged leviathans of the family that produced Webster's Third in 1961. As Dr. Woolf put it, "Editors were writing slips to the W4."

Thesaurus

In the harsh soil of contemporary language blooms the verbiferous thesaurus, giving color to thought, fragrance to expression, shade to meaning, and poetic license to copywriters.

Latest of the species was—*The Doubleday Roget's Thesaurus in Dictionary Form.* On its dust jacket the work hymns itself as "Completely new," a panegyric recalling the effusions of last year's *Webster's Collegiate Thesaurus.* That book, published by Merriam-Webster, called itself "The first totally new thesaurus in over 120 years," as though its editor, Mairé Weir Kay, had not acknowledged in the introduction that her staff "freely consulted existent thesauruses."

None of this should induce the publisher of *Roget's International Thesaurus* to stop describing it as "MOST COMPLETE." Nor should it prevent *The Original Roget's Thesaurus of English Words and Phrases* from continuing to seek its own margin of distinction as "The only Thesaurus that gives parts of speech in both text and index."

Small wonder that the Original Roget's lists the senses of *competition* as "imitation, opposition, contention, sale, jealousy." The market is immense. With upwards of 50 thesauri in print, only the most discriminating publicist hesitates before extolling the company's thesaurus as first of its kind or most blessed of its breed. In the 30 years since its first edition, Pocket Books has sold over 12 million copies of its thesauruses; in 20 years Signet has sold almost nine million.

It was Peter Mark Roget who created the thesaurus arrangement and gave the species his name. Roget, who was born in London, eased into lexicography by studying medicine, writing on science, and inventing a slide-rule and pocket chessboard. After retirement as Secretary of the Royal Society, he amplified an old word-classification system he had earlier devised, and in 1852 it was published as a thesaurus.

Roget described his device as the opposite of a dictionary. With a dictionary, one knows the word and seeks its meaning; with a thesaurus, one knows the meaning and seeks the word. As a contemporary thesaurus editor put it: "When you have a dictionary you look up a word you want; when you have a thesaurus you look up a word you don't want."

Inspired by notions of scientific order and philosophic comprehensiveness, Roget imposed a six-fold division on vocabulary—Abstract Relations, Space, Matter, Intellect, Volition and Affections—and listed words in 1,000 subdivisions. Much was arbitrary and repetitive. "I have always preferred to subject myself to the imputation of redundance," he said, "rather than incur the reproach of insufficiency." Eventually, by addition of an index, it became unnecessary for readers to master the six-fold way or pay it any heed at all.

Roget died in 1869. His son edited succeeding editions,

then his grandson took over, and eventually the family sold its rights to Longmans, publisher of the original edition. Longmans still publishes the direct descendant of the original in London, and St. Martin's Press puts it out here, Americanized, "revised and modernized," and distinguished as "the Original."

A collateral descendant—this one not "Original" but "International"—is published here by Thomas Y. Crowell, and the original, international bickering between Longmans and Crowell, over publication rights, has given way to unabridged transatlantic amity and forbearance.

Both companies watch helplessly as others crowd the market, advertising latter-day entries with verve and audacity, and arranging their works not only as Roget did but also alphabetically.

Sisson's Synonyms, published by Prentice-Hall, and compiled by A.F. Sisson, is a contender in the abecedarian ranks, and though the title has the outspoken advantage of alliteration, Sisson's name is less renowned than Roget's.

Laird's Promptory was a 1948 entry, named for *its* compiler, Charlton Laird. He took *promptory* from the Latin *promptorium* (storehouse), and proclaimed: "For a new kind of book, a new kind of name!"

Professor Laird, now emeritus at the University of Nevada, went on to edit *Webster's New World Thesaurus*, one of the many word books profiting from the fact that "Webster" belongs to anyone who wants it, be he Laird or commoner. "Roget" is also available to all, and some day the world will surely see a "Webster's Roget" or at least a "Roget's Webster."

Merriam-Webster's *Webster's Collegiate Thesaurus* boasts that it stands above the rest and offers "synonym lists that contain only exact synonyms." The editors, having reduced words to elements of meaning, omit an enormous number of simple as well as difficult words. Thus, for example, they have not listed *peace* (Doubleday does, to say nothing of the Original and International), allegedly because they could find no exact synonyms. And though one may war against the enemy, the noun *war* is not listed in this Webster's, though Doubleday admits it. There is no *pogrom* or *ghetto* in Webster's list; Doubleday has *ghetto* but no *pogrom*. The Original and the International have both words.

Sidney I. Landau, editor of the Doubleday Thesaurus, several years ago published an analysis of lexicographic treatment of the commonest term for sexual intercourse, but his thesaurus cedes the territory to competitors. *Webster's Collegiate Thesaurus* gives figurative senses of the common vulgarity, but slips away from its literal sense. The Original and International omit the word entirely. There is not even a listing for *adultery* in the Webster or the Doubleday, but the Original and the International welcome it.

Webster's Collegiate Thesaurus is god-less, though it lists *goddamn, godless, godlike, godly, God's acre* and *godsend.* Asked to explain the dearth of god, Dr. Kay said that she felt the subject was too "touchy" for her thesaurus.

Doubleday has 13 listings under *god.* The Original and the International are crowded with gods Greek, Roman, Norse, Hindu, Egyptian, Aboriginal and then some.

Devil gets his due in *Webster's Collegiate Thesaurus,* which includes *Clootie, Old Gooseberry* and *Old Scratch.* Doubleday treads warily, restricting itself to more familiar appellations such as *Prince of Darkness* and *Tempter.* The Original has a rich cargo, including *Old Gentleman* and *angel of the bottomless pit,* and the International welcomes *Old Harry* and *Old Bendy.*

Under *headgear*, the Original bears many hats: half a column of small print includes *puggaree, tarboosh, calash, morion, wideawake* and *petasos*. The International offers a haberdasher's delectation, including *ruman, scraper, sola topee* and *wimple*.

Has Doubleday blown its lid? There is no listing for *hat*, and the word does not even grace the entries for *cap*. *Webster's Collegiate Thesaurus* enters the fray hat-less and headgear-less, and there is not even a listing for *toupee, hairpiece,* or *wig* except as rebuke.

In the Original and International, *inflation* gets full-blown treatment. There's no *inflation* listed in Doubleday, though *inflate* is there. Webster's omits *inflation* but includes *inflate* and *inflated*, unrelated to currency.

All this delighted Patrick Barrett, editor-in-chief of the reference department at Crowell's, publisher of the International, when he studied *Webster's Collegiate Thesaurus*. Such is the scholar's passion for neutrality that he quickly concluded the other company's work was inferior.

He pointed out, for example, that the Collegiate Webster's, which has entries for *pig, box, pit, pudding* and *ship* (though none for *boat*) ignored *pig* as animal, *box* as container, *pit* as hole or mine or stone of fruit, *pudding* as dessert, and *ship* as any sort of seaworthy noun. Doubleday recognizes *pig* as swine, piglet, hog, sow, shoat and boar; it accepts *box* as container; it admits *pit* as hole, mine and stone of fruit; but it finishes off without *pudding*. While saluting *ship* as vessel, craft and watercraft but not as boat it greets *boat* as watercraft, vessel, craft and ship.

Crowell, publisher of the International, was naturally preparing to publish its new edition, and according to the ode it was preparing, this *Roget's International Thesaurus* would not be "new" (Merriam-Webster's word) or "completely new" (Doubleday's). It would be "newest." Of course, it would also be "largest, and most useful," but in this field, that rarely goes without saying.

CLERKS TO
THE LANGUAGE

Eric Partridge

Eric Partridge's first collection of essays was entitled *Words, Words, Words.*

How could it have been anything else? For more years than it is comfortable to remember or seemly to forget, he has served his Queen's English and its cousins abroad as dauntless guardian of the majestic and occasionally frolicsome English tongue. In dictionaries massive, glossaries exhaustive, articles frothy, reviews engaging, he has put words in their place, communicating delight in well-ordered vocabularies and impatience with collections of letters artlessly posing as words.

As was said of him almost 60 years ago, Partridge is always game. Edmund Wilson, who also knew a thing or two about words, hailed Partridge as "the word king," and others acknowledged his primacy by calling him "the dictionary man" or "the word man."

Although he took Wilson's tribute in good spirit, the other titles wearied him—almost beyond words. "Clichés," he called them.

A Dictionary of Clichés is one of his standard works.

"Useful and almost readable," he called it, and spoke of "that excellent blood sport: cliché-hunting." (At this point in time, the cliché that displeases him most is "in this day and age.")

He is offended when confused with a computer or a lexicographers' cartel. "(I am) none of those soulless or diabolical things," he said, insisting that he preferred to do his own work and to make his own mistakes.

In 1950 Partridge became the first scholar to write a historical and comprehensive dictionary of the underworld. In *Shakespeare's Bawdy* he was the first scholar to treat the vast underbelly of Shakespeare's language sympathetically and—as he put it—"sensibly," indeed to treat it as an integral, self-contained subject.

A Dictionary of Slang and Unconventional English, which has gone through many editions, put slang on the linguistic map and helped make its study respectable. Partridge followed this debut with *The Dictionary of Historical Slang, A Smaller Slang Dictionary* ("aseptic," he called it), and *Slang Today & Yesterday.*

Opting to make his position self-effacingly plain by using the third person, Partridge said: "He's done a lot to rid common speech—and, come to that, 'the four-letter words'—of the stigma of being unspeakable and, especially, unwritable. As distinct from those who, eager to urge others in the fight for verbal freedom, are too cowardly or too cautious to take a risk themselves, he has—'to coin a phrase'—suffered in the cause. In 1928 he was prosecuted for printing a novel that contained *Christ!* as an oath and *bugger* as a mere synonym for *chap* or *fellow.*"

Partridge was seven years old when he learned to use a dictionary, in his native, rural New Zealand, and he was only eight when he learned how devilish a dictionary could be.

His father and a visiting farmer were arguing about the herds and bees, and Partridge *père* identified one insect as a "humble" bee. "Bumble" bee, insisted the visitor. Secretly the son looked it up and found *bumble bee,* but no *humble bee.* Later he consulted a bigger dictionary and discovered that neither disputant was altogether right: *humble bee* was perhaps earlier, and *bumble bee* was no less honorable.

The family moved to Australia, where wildlife, vocabulary, and syntax differed from New Zealand's, and Partridge—age 13—bought a notebook and entered new words. In the Australian army in World War I he learned more, some printable. Then he went to Oxford and learned to speak, not Standard English, but what he called "one of the Modified Standards"—clear, not dulcet or tony or produced as though the nose had replaced the larynx as vocal organ.

He landed in lexicography footnotes first, with an appendix to his M.A. thesis—listing neologisms committed by English romantic poets. Then John Brophy, a novelist, suggested collaboration on *Songs and Slang of the British Soldier.* One contributor was the soldier who became Field Marshal Lord Wavell.

In the British army, during World War II, Partridge decided to make short work of abbreviations there and compiled an abbreviation guide. Switching to the Royal Air Force, he continued his linguistic campaign and produced *A Dictionary of RAF Slang.* Then, with help from brothers-in-arms, he elaborated *A Dictionary of Forces' Slang, 1939–1945.*

Substantial works in these ranks are known by their initials. O.E.D. is the *Oxford English Dictionary*, earlier called N.E.D.—for *New English Dictionary*. M.E.U. is universally accepted for *Modern English Usage*. Partridge's D.S.U.E. became current for *A Dictionary of Slang and Unconventional English*.

In 1958 Partridge wrote a centenary celebration of Henry Watson Fowler, author of the classic M.E.U. "There is only one Fowler," Partridge proclaimed, and went on to deal with charges that M.E.U. contains many faults. "Of course it does!" he noted. "Every worthwhile book contains many faults, and every worthwhile writer commits them." He later committed this insight to maximum application: "He who never makes mistakes makes nothing."

When Partridge wanted to write *Usage & Abusage* (U.&A.), his publisher argued that it would be suicide to try to compete with M.E.U. But another publisher saw life in the idea, and the book—more popular in approach than Fowler's—came out in the United States in 1942 and in Britain five years later. It has gone into edition after edition, printing after printing.

Partridge puts his books into weight categories, as though each were ready to enter the ring. *Name This Child* was frankly lightweight, and one of the chattier references deals with his own first name, Eric: "Literally it is perhaps 'ever king.' ... By 'Johns' and 'moms' and 'Dons,' it is often-...despised as pretty-pretty." One of the stalwart heavyweights was *Origins: A Short Etymological Dictionary of Modern English*, which he described as "scholarly—readable—refreshing—brilliantly organized."

These outbursts are interspersed with effusions of modesty, such as: "I don't regard myself—please excuse the switch from the impersonal *he* to the egotistic *I*—as an expert at anything; probably rightly, for I'm pretty sure I'm not."

Partridge is not a university professor and does not think of himself as learned. A scholar takes too much for granted; an outsider can see things fresh. He bristles when anyone is called a "gifted amateur" and re-bristles when he comes across those he calls "career boys" in fields academic, literary, artistic, or theatrical.

He admits to being occasionally at a loss for words: "Like everybody else, yes I am! Can usually find *some* words—that's easy; to find the utterly right word—right for the subject and right for the occasion—is occasionally more difficult, if not (to me, anyway) impossible."

Sometimes it takes little to get him started, for example, the suggestion that he must have some theories about language. "Theories?" he rejoined, and reverted to the third person to tell everything about *that:* "He hasn't any particular theories about language, except the belief, rather than theory, that, in the study of any and every aspect of language, that scholar who forgets that language was created by people, not in a laboratory, and that it lives—or at one time lived—only by and in people, and that its entire *raison d'être* is to communicate, to express and serve a civilization, not to exemplify some grammatical or philological theory, is strangely lacking in a sense of proportion and even in common sense."

"Words are doing fine!" he insisted. "By that I mean language is. But then it always *will* be. Words deserving to be retained and conserved and remembered—honored, if you prefer it so—will be; the silly words and phrases, like the pretentious ones, will die—some of 'em die with a commendable celerity. In the main, that is. There are always the apparently inexplicable exceptions of apparent injustice and regrettable luck.

"Expressions that offend me are clichés in general; all slipshoddery; unnecessary neologisms; obscene words and phrases that are dragged in for the sake of obscenity—not those which are integral—entirely natural—to dialogue or other matter."

He works on his preferences at home in the English countryside. Slow to anger, an imperfect demon when roused, Partridge is usually equable and always determined. When he was tussling with *A Dictionary of Catch Phrases*, British and American, from the sixteenth century to the present day, a New Year's greeting to friends was a printed, four-page progress report on the dictionary, with barely enough room at the end for a scrawled personal message.

When he was asked to suggest a bouquet of phrases appropriate for greeting a gentleman of letters commemorating 80 years of struggle with those letters, he replied: "The only phrase or adage I can think of as being in the least adequate and relevant is the motto of the Salvation Army, 'Keep *on* keeping on.' The unkind might propose 'Evidence of a misspent life.' Anyway, I have, in the main, enjoyed it—and hope to go on doing so for a while. I'm one of those bloody fools who don't know when they're beaten."

Clarence Barnhart

Clarence L. Barnhart, of Clarence L. Barnhart Inc., runs a company that makes dictionaries. Now that he is almost 80 years old and it is over 30, Mr. Barnhart occasionally forgets accomplishments past, but what lies ahead is clear in a tome on his office shelf. "Future Projects" speaks volumes.

Mr. Barnhart plans a British-American pronouncing dictionary, an updated version of *The Barnhart Dictionary of New English Since 1963* and a history of 20th century lexicography. He is considering a dictionary of pocket-size and another based on words in 500 important books since 1900. He is even studying ways to treat words that mean one thing in America and another, say, in the Soviet Union—words like *democracy*.

"We consider ourselves secretaries for the English language," he says of his enterprise in which popular usage dictates editors' choices and choices then dictate usage. "I take the stand that an editor should include his opinions about usage, so long as he labels them as his."

"What is an editor?" he pursues rhetorically, replying:

"Somebody who doesn't know what to do in the world."

During preliminary years of indecision, he worked his way through the University of Chicago, studying English literature and expecting to teach it, though afflicted with an interest in science and philosophy. He taught in a one-room schoolhouse and even served as Minister in a single-minded church. Then he made the mistake of reading Thomas H. Huxley and a few others and, as he says, "They fixed me up for good."

He got a job in the shipping room of Scott Foresman, a Chicago publisher, then transferred to the dictionary department and to arguments with Edward L. Thorndike, an educational psychologist advising on lexicography. "Dr. Thorndike got mad and I got mad, because we were discussing principles," Mr. Barnhart said, "and that formed the basis of a long friendship."

Collaboration brought 50,000 written comments to Dr. Thorndike, and then—when the first dictionary was ready—a rhymed couplet: "Glory be to C.L.B. and me/I now will have a little time free."

In 1944 the War Department directed C.L.B. to produce a dictionary of army terms, and he confused staff ranks by giving privates command over majors. "They knew more," he explained. His parting heresy was finishing the dictionary within the deadline and returning several thousand dollars to the government.

Random House then asked him to do an American dictionary. "What those boys wanted to do was take the Concise Oxford and steal it," he said. "So we made the *American College Dictionary*. They put half a million dollars into it instead of the 75,000 they wanted to put into it."

When Random House asked whose name to put on the

title page, Mr. Barnhart replied, "Why don't you put the name of the man who made it?"

"I rather think vanity is sometimes just as strong a motive as profit," he suggested later.

The A.C.D. was the first college dictionary to use linguistics—a method inspired by the University of Chicago's Leonard Bloomfield, who astonished Mr. Barnhart by refusing to accept money for his help.

When Random House put old furniture into Mr. Barnhart's department, he did not need a definition of company intent. "I could have fought," he said, "but I didn't like corporate fighting and I didn't like corporations, so I set up my own."

His wife Frances was skeptical about independence, but she silently pitched in as company bookkeeper, and she still balances the books when the regular bookkeeper is on vacation. Sons Robert and David are editors in the family corporation.

Since he disliked working for others, Mr. Barnhart takes pains to please those who work for him. The office is an intriguing, complex labyrinth of bookshelves and cabinets crowded with reference volumes and word-citation computer cards. Work cubicles are sequestered within the labyrinth; an employee could lose himself in his work, or simply en route. There is no time clock to punch or explanations to make in case of absence. "You have to give employees in professional places the sense of freedom they'd have if they were working on their own," Mr. Barnhart said.

His handyman became an excellent alphabetizer, and the typist proved a fine etymologist. Mr. Barnhart discusses work with his editors instead of simply handing it out. Names of editors go on books, and they get royalties. Sol

Steinmetz, who came in 1961 from Merriam-Webster, still feels guilty about the joy he gets working chez Barnhart at lexicography—what Samuel Johnson described as drudgery.

Clarence Barnhart himself can hardly wait—seven days a week—to get going. Daily he rises at six to spend the next four hours—more on Sunday—netting words of novelty and interest from a morning newspaper. Journals of right and left satisfy his thirst for opinion and knowledge of linguistic extremes. He used to subscribe to a paper from Fiji, and he was amused when weeks went by and it didn't even mention the United States, center of the universe.

He takes pains not to feel overwhelmed by words and works. "You do what you can and you do the best you can while you do it," he said.

"The hours you put in are just fantastic, and whether you're an editor or an author you're a peon. You have to contribute your own time to make good books, and in today's publishing I miss a drive to get the books just right. What's published is no longer decided by editors—it's decided by salesmen."

When he was only 75 years old, Mr. Barnhart had open-heart surgery, and then returned rosy-cheeked and more cheerful than ever. "They took my heart out and put it in again," he said. "I feel like a new edition."

Noah Webster

Noah Webster spent a lifetime (1758- 1843) taming disorders of vocabulary and anarchies of usage, and when his *American Dictionary of the English Language* came out, in 1828, he considered his struggle victorious—he had domesticated English.

With his dictionary long since absorbed into larger and even greater works, he is remembered as the father of American lexicography, his very name synonymous with "dictionary."

A man of severe mien and stubborn industry, Webster divided his allegiance between conservatism and audacity. Long after the fashion changed, he went about in black knee breeches and black silk stockings; long before America gained its cultural independence he fought to free the nation from what he termed blind and servile veneration of European authorities. "America must be as independent in *literature* as she is in *politics*," he declared, "as famous for *arts* as for *arms*."

Until Webster's assault, the great lexical authority was Samuel Johnson's 1755 dictionary, a work Webster condemned:

Many of its words were not English—adversable, advesperate, adjugate, agriculation, abstrude, injudicable, spicosity, crapulence, morigerous, tenebrosity, balbucinate, illachrymable.

Merely because the likes of Shakespeare used them, vulgarities abounded—fishify, jackalent, parma-citty, jeggumbob, conjabble.

Definitions showed "want of discrimination." *Fraud*, for example, was defined as deceit, cheat, trick, artifice, subtility and stratagem, though one could use tricks, artifice, subtility and stratagems without fraud and could be deceived without being defrauded.

Americanisms were condemned to exile, and so were many of the most common words of English.

As to etymology, there were hardly words to qualify it.

Webster's own roots were in a Connecticut farm childhood. Hoping to inspire youth with an abhorrence of vice and a love of virtue, he struggled to make a living as a rural schoolteacher. When he considered the English language and American education, he felt it his mission to improve the one and correct the other.

To improve his own condition he eventually studied law, even practiced it for a while, but his heart belonged less to righting wrongs than to writing right. He therefore set to work and compiled a spelling book designed to reform pronunciation and syllabication, and to "extirpate the improprieties and vulgarisms...the abuses and corruptions."

Between 1783 and 1900 his spelling text sold an estimated 70 million copies, endowing its creator with the inalienable right to be known as America's Schoolteacher.

Webster consolidated the right with **a grammar (1784)** following his principle that "grammar is founded on language, and not language on grammar," and then with a reader, an anthology comprising mainly American selections and thus suitably nationalistic as well as moralistic.

Webster found that temporal rewards eluded him. He was a dismal businessman, and was forever signing away future royalties in exchange for pittances of ready cash.

Determined to right the balance, he pioneered in the delicate humiliations of the author's tour, lecturing on language while lobbying for copyright protection, and attacking the competition while puffing his own product. Scientific work might attract attention, he said, but it casts light only in an obscure study, while his humble spelling volume, for example, "like a star casts its beams equally upon the peasant and the monarch."

In his glosses, modesty was rarely underlined. When a critic objected to mistakes in the spelling book, Webster said he had published it "for real scholars to criticize and for fools to carp at." He was repeatedly castigated for insufferable vanity, and even ridiculed as "coxcomb-general of the United States." One account had it that when Benjamin Rush greeted Webster by exclaiming "I congratulate you on your arrival to Philadelphia," Webster rejoined "You may congratulate Philadelphia on the occasion."

To the woman who became his bride, Webster wrote letters brimming with characteristic passion: "The eyes of America are upon me, and having made my appearance upon the stage, I must act my part well or lose both my reputation and my prospects."

Benjamin Franklin consulted him about alphabet reform; George Washington sought his advice on pedagogy;

Jefferson dismissed him as "a mere pedagogue of limited understanding and very strong prejudices and party associations." Webster blithely continued to lecture on his political principles, to preside over unsuccessful opinion journals, to serve in the state legislature, and then some, for his interests drew him far afield. He wrote Washington: "The approbation given to my theory of vegetable manure by so experienced and judicious a cultivator of the earth as your Excellency is a flattering circumstance..." "I am unwilling to lose an opportunity," he wrote another authority, "of adding my mite to your stock of materials for illustrating the causes of winds." Though no physician and hardly a scientist either, he wrote a two-volume work on epidemic and pestilential diseases.

Try though he might, he was unable to cure himself of the plague endemic to lexicography—fiat vs. custom, prescription vs. passivity. If critics refused to accept popular usage, Webster argued that custom sanctioned it; when conservatives rejected innovation, Webster complained that people were ready to correct errors everywhere except in language.

Canons to the right of him, canons to the left of him, Webster plunged onward. In 1800 he announced his plan to produce a series of American dictionaries that would be superior to all others. The first came out in 1806, with more words than Dr. Johnson saw fit to include, and some spellings he certainly would have rejected, such as *imagin, catcal, soop* and *catastrophy*.

School abridgments followed, but Webster was more concerned with the ultimate dictionary and the demands of survival. Oppressed by debt, he moved his family from New Haven to Amherst, in 1812, to save money. When he offered the public a chance to subscribe to his large dictionary in advance, for $10, few responded. He worked on, obsessed by his aims, chagrined by his trials, and foolhardy enough to offer a suit of clothes to anyone who could fully explain the word *by*.

To prepare his etymologies, he spent ten years compiling a "Synopsis of the Affinities of Twenty Languages," including such esoteric tongues as Arabic, Samaritan, Chaldaic, Hebrew and Ethiopic. To consult material unavailable in America, he borrowed $1,000 from a married daughter and went off to continue his research in Europe. Finally, in Cambridge, England, he completed the body of his dictionary.

"When I had come to the last word," he wrote, "I was seized with a trembling, which made it somewhat difficult to hold my pen steady for writing. The cause seems to have been the thought that I might not then live to finish the work..."

The great book had some 70,000 entries, and included words of science and industry, colloquialisms, Americanisms, new forms with new meanings (*accompaniment, appreciate, editorial*), one Webster neologism (*demoralize*) and a single example of the first person, illustrating the use of *witness*: "I *witnessed* the ceremonies in New York, with which the ratification of the constitution was celebrated in 1788."

Webster's definitions outshone those of his predecessors, but his examples of usage struggled under the burden of that first person's pieties: "The *love* of God is the first duty of man," "*Patriotism* is...the noblest passion that animates a man in the character of a citizen."

Determined to restore what he described as original

and superior orthography, Webster studded his work with spellings whose day had not returned—*ake, crum, fether, imagin, wimmen, wo.* But some of his preferences took hold: *center* (rather than *centre*), *music* (musick), *plow* (plough).

In pronunciation, his ear was fallible: "ax" rather than "ask," "deef" not "deaf," "furder" instead of "further." And despite his toil on affinities, many of his derivations proved more fancy than fact, victim of the undeveloped state of early 19th century philology.

But as Webster promised, the work was a considerable improvement over rivals, and a first edition of 2,500 ($20 for two folio volumes) sold out in about a year. Even in England—edition of 3,000 copies—the dictionary was accepted as authoritative.

"Noah's Ark," as it came to be known, proved hardy enough to survive a deluge of criticism. When one dissident expressed astonishment that *demijohn* wasn't in the dictionary, Webster suggested that he "compile a work of that size, examine 70,000 words, trace many of them through five, ten, fifteen languages and collect all the senses in which they are used, thousands of which are in no common English dictionary."

At age 70, Webster should have reaped the harvest of his labors, but his American publisher, through unfortunate speculations, went bankrupt, tying up the royalties. When Webster published his own edition, in 1841, he had to mortgage his home to pay for printing.

After Webster's death, George and Charles Merriam bought the unsold stock and went headlong into the dictionary business. The name Webster is in the public domain, but the Merriam-Webster company prides itself on enjoying, as one author put it, the apostolic succession. To mark the 150th anniversary of the great original, the company made plans to donate its archives to Yale's Beinecke Library, and an 1828 dictionary to the White House, where Noah's Ark could do wonders for the reigning accent.

Sherman Kuhn—Middle English Dictionary

With disdain for editorial mortality and other deadlines, the *Middle English Dictionary* project was taking forever to get to *Z*. But the Mellon Foundation suddenly gave the project $950,000—and a deadline only seven years away. Swelling from a part-time staff of nine to an industrial enterprise of 18—half of them full-time—the University of Michigan project in Ann Arbor moved from fusty cubicles in weathered Angell Hall to modern, grander quarters. That was more than enough to disorient the veterans of this 50-year project. When the editors trooped downstairs to Bicycle Jim's for an inaugural lunch, Richard L. McKelvey, one of the editors, mused: "I do hope nobody steals the letter W while we're away."

The archives began with a loan from the Oxford English Dictionary staff of a million word-slips, with quotations, drawn from medieval English. More than a hundred scholarly volunteers added citations from their reading, and eventually there were over three million slips arranged alphabetically, including one full box marked "buttok to bye-bye." The Michigan staff supplemented the stock by reading Latin documents in which Middle English (1100 to 1500) surfaces, for example when the scribe does not know the Latin for *fire tong* or *muck fork*. Then, 40 years ago, MED–men cleared the way with a survey identifying subdialects in four major dialect areas of Middle English, Northern, Midland, Kentish and Southern (Chaucer's English was East Midland).

All dialects were derived from Old English, spoken by the Anglo-Saxons, akin to Low German and Dutch, less closely related to High German and Scandinavian languages. There are many borrowings from Latin, and from Norse because of Danish and Norwegian forays in the 9th and 11th centuries.

With the Norman conquest, in 1066, French influence spread rapidly. In *Ivanhoe*, Walter Scott glosses the distinctions between coarse Anglo-Saxon of indigenous swineherds and cultured French of Normans to the manoir born. Animals on the hoof are rounded up in Old English (sow, ox), meat on the table is elevated to derivations from French (pork, beef). As the jester puts it to the swineherd: "...when the brute lives, and is in the charge of a Saxon slave, she goes by her Saxon name; but becomes a Norman...when she is carried to the castle hall to feast among the nobles."

French also provided legal and literary terms. Divine love cloaks itself in Latin raiment; expressions of courtly love don wan coats of French.

In 1952 the first fascicle of words was published, covering *E* up to *endelonges* (along). *A*, *B* and parts of *C* and *D* had been edited under an old plan, so editors back-tracked to expand the entries. At the rate of about two 128-page fascicles annually, and 48 thus far (6,315 double-columned pages), the dictionary was mid-course, puffing toward *N*.

Each fascicle is published in 2,000 copies, to cover the demand from institutions. Two copies go to Poland and one each to Moscow and Peking. "There used to be a copy which went out to what they called Leopoldville, in the country now called Zaire," said Professor Sherman M. Kuhn, the fifth editor of MED. "I hope nothing happened to it in the rioting there. I hope somebody's using it."

About every five years the University of Michigan Press publishes a volume incorporating the latest fascicles. When Volume 5, *I* to *L*, came out, the editors had forgotten to include a title page, so they sent subscribers a loose one. "We don't start a new volume often enough," explained Professor Kuhn. "If we did it every week we'd remember the title page."

Complications lurk in every letter and notably in common verbs such as *to be* and *to make*—the latter makes up 42 columns in fascicle 47. "It's an awful lot of space," said Professor Kuhn, "but we could have made it 20 pages longer." He is the specialist in complexity, and inevitably winds up preparing entries for tricky blighters like *do*.

At the other end of the scale is what the Greeks, who had two words for it, called *hapax legomenon*, which the MED staff domesticates as "oncers." These are words occurring only once in the literature. An example is *malliacionne* (hammering), its single, crucial occurrence in: "And to soune of thas hamers and fabricacionne, Cristis prayere is liknd and his crucifioures malliacionne."

Tilting at the lists produces a bounty of linguistic ingenuity, as with the French-derived *mal-toter*—bearer of evil tottings, thus collector of taxes on ale; or with "make hit taper-wise waxinge," as in whittling a fishing rod.

Man is first presented in the sense of human being,

defined as "a person, man or woman," the common sense in Old and Middle English. Attempts by modern women to limit the uses of *man* rouse Professor Kuhn to irascible heights.

He speaks from the collective eminence of a staff commanding not only Old, Middle and Modern English, but Latin (classical, medieval and church), classical Greek, French (old and modern), Dutch (middle and modern), Old Welsh, Old Icelandic, Old Saxon, German (old high, middle high, modern), Italian, Spanish (not much help), Chinese (even less help) and Irish (old and middle). "We're kind of weak in modern Irish," said Professor Kuhn. "We could also use an Arabist."

Those native to English have an advantage over late comers. A Korean formerly on the staff submitted a definition of the Middle English forms of *juggler* which read in part: "a performer of lying wonders." That was dropped from the final proof.

"This project takes nimble footwork, a touch of insanity and perseverance in the face of defeat," said Professor Kuhn. "Etymology is the field in which we're defeated most frequently. We try Old English—it's not there. We try Old Norse—we're foiled. We try Middle Dutch—not a sign of it. Just about the time we're ready to give up we find something that could be the ancestor of it in Old Welsh. I'm bogged down at the moment with *miltz*, which is spelled about 40 different ways and means mercy or grace or favor or kindness and a few other things probably.

"You reach the point where you just don't know what the word means in a certain context. You have to admit defeat when you're defeated, especially if it's one of those *oncers*."

Occasionally MED stammers in perplexity, as with the entry for *mamering*—"?Mumbling, ?muttering, ?babbling." In dire cases, stubborn puzzlers, editors employ what Professor Bernard Van't Hul calls a "confessional definition," for example, "a plant of some kind."

"The largest challenges to sustained production are the tedium of necessary trivia and the novice's temptation to indulge in excessive nuance," he noted.

Twice he has almost despaired. *"Mead* (meadow, reward, potion, inhabitant of ancient Medea) staggered me and *life* almost did me in," he said. "My insomnia was riddled with insights into the slippery blackguards. I suffer from the Hamlet syndrome—shall I end it all, or attack the problem again later?"

"That's better than the Gertrude syndrome—marrying the wrong definition," noted Mr. McKelvey consolingly.

He came to MED more than 35 years ago and slowly acquired fluency in deciphering foggy, medieval scribbles. Two years went to reading a single book—a translation into Middle English of *De Proprietatibus Rerum*, an encyclopedia introducing such pedestrian wonders as a race of one-legged people who use their foot to shade their head.

Signal events are much rarer in the life of the editors. The project's most luminous moment came in Ross MacDonald's mystery *The Dark Tunnel*, when a body falls from the Middle English Dictionary office in a college town called Arbana. Stalwarts have grown gray in devotion to duty, and one of the ironies of their fate is that their new office formerly housed the university's gerontology project. Mr. McKelvey thought the gerontology sign on the door would now be superfluous. "When people come in," he said, "they're going to know it's gerontology without being told."

"I remember when I came here in 1948," said Professor Kuhn. "I had big plans for what I would do as soon as we finished the dictionary. The years went by, and here we are in the middle of *M*. There have been times when I've wished it was a project I could finish in my lifetime. Now the idea of finishing it in seven years frightens me."

FASHIONS OF USAGE

American Heritage Dictionary—I

A dictionary should be an embarrassment of riches, not a richness of embarrassments, but nowadays it is a little of both.

In 1961, *Webster's Third New International Dictionary* was praised and damned as permissive. By the time Random House published a dictionary, in 1966, it was harder to tell permissiveness from strict construction. In *The American Heritage Dictionary*, the distinction is approached even more warily.

Since democracy is part of the American heritage, the dictionary's editors set up a "usage panel" of 104 writers, editors, professors, and public figures to vote on specific expressions and general usage. On occasion the panelists were surprisingly permissive. Thus, Dwight MacDonald, the author-critic, wrote: "I favor dropping 'whom' altogether as a needless refinement."

But Katherine Anne Porter, the novelist, would not hear of allowing *who* for *whom*. She said it was "Acceptable in speech, if you don't mind who hears you." Acceptable no matter who's listening, ruled the panel, but unacceptable in writing.

Miss Porter decided that *O.K.* was a slip of fools: "Any form, any spelling is a detestable vulgarity, entirely offensive to the ear. I have never spoken the word in my life, and I loathe the sound of it." But the expression as a noun was O.K.'d by 57 per cent, as an adjective by 23 per cent, as a verb by 42 per cent and as an adverb by 20 per cent.

Confronted by *enthuse*, Mr. MacDonald declared: "By God, let's hold the line on this one!" John Fischer of *Harper's* said simply: "There is no such word." Only a quarter of his colleagues disagreed.

When Mr. MacDonald faced *fortuitous* as a substitute for *fortunate* he dug in his cleats: "Users of a language must learn it before they can change it; simple illiteracy is no basis for linguistic evolution." Fifteen per cent voted for such illiteracy.

The split infinitive was welcomed cautiously. Banning it, said Morris Bishop, author and past president of the Modern Language Association, is a "mere symbol of gentility, like the prohibition of cutting lettuce with a fork." The panel voted to more or less accept split infinitives, with each use to be separately examined.

For use in speech, "it is me" won 60 per cent of the votes, but only 22 per cent for use in writing. Joseph A. Brandt, a professor emeritus of journalism at the University of California at Los Angeles, called it "grammatical incest."

On the use of *above* as an adjective (as in "the above figures") and as a noun (as in "the above is incorrect"), Red Smith, the sports columnist, commented: "It's business-letter English, meaning acceptable and undesirable." A majority agreed to accept "above" as an adjective, but not as a noun.

Did the panel object to *gift* as a transitive verb? Mr.

Smith observed: "If he gifts her wisely, she should host him warmly, which could be immoral." Six per cent were ready to accept such a gift, and 18 per cent were prepared to go along with Mr. Smith's use of *host*.

The verb *escalate*, used transitively in the sense of stepping up an effort, provoked forceful rejoinders, but three-quarters of the panel voted for it. Richard H. Rovere of *The New Yorker* said: "This one has been settled by force of arms and may as well be accepted as a useful term."

"Yes, dammit!" agreed Russell Lynes of *Harper's* magazine, while Bruce Catton, the historian, said: "No, but I suppose nothing can be done about it." Mr. Lynes, confronted with the suffix *-wise*, as in *populationwise*, replied "Nowise!"

Isaac Asimov, a biochemist who writes history and science fiction, refused to see *finalize* in any of his pasts or futures. John Bainbridge, the author, was more tolerant: "To be used only facetiously, except by bureaucrats and generals." It was Asimov, nine to one.

Professor Jacques Barzun of Columbia University decried *descalate* for *de-escalate*. "I would desprecate it," he said, and so would 93 per cent of the panel.

He flailed at *flaunt* as a substitute for *flout* (defy with contempt). "This is an appalling question, for if latitude is given in this case, all malapropisms are justified: Just cut the dictionary in half and double the synonyms." Only nine per cent opposed his view.

There was no one like Dr. Barzun when it came to anti-latitudinarianism. On *regime* as a synonym for *administration*, as in "Kennedy regime," he said: "No, and cut out 'dynasty' in the same contexts: these are technical terms, you blasted non-historians!" Seventy-two per cent took no offense, and voted against Dr. Barzun's view.

On *premiere* as a verb ("The conductor will premiere two works.") Professor Barzun asked: "And derrière them at the same time?" Eighty-six per cent turned their backs on that.

David Ogilvy, an adman—or rather, advertising executive—was optimistic about ending *hopefully*, as in, "Hopefully, I'll get a raise this year." "If your dictionary could kill this horror, and do nothing else," Mr. Ogilvy wrote, "it would be worth publishing." Fifty-six per cent of the panel joined his plea for capital punishment.

Personality, in the sense of well-known person, squeezed through with 57 per cent. "Very common and bad," insisted William K. Zinsser, the humorous non-personality and critic. "Help stamp out 'personality'!"

Berton Roueché of *The New Yorker* was ready to send *senior citizen* into permanent retirement. "I'd as soon use 'underprivileged' for 'poor,' " he remarked, "or any other social-science Choctaw." But 47 per cent voted to admit *senior citizen* to the republic of letters.

John Ciardi, the poet, asserted that the use of *shall* was "pretentious" and that *will* was "the natural response of the American voice box."

"Hear! Hear!" cried 62 percent.

A correct appraisal of the first person's role was crucial to the whole exercise. Said Dr. Asimov: "My own neologisms are perfectly acceptable. It is those of others to which I object." Wallace Stegner, the author, noted: "My objections, as well as my approvals, strike me as nearly totally irrational."

The panel reached unanimity only once—when it examined *simultaneous* as an adverb, as in "The referendum was conducted simultaneous with the election." All at once, everybody voted no.

"You are still going strong," Sheridan Baker, professor of English at the University of Michigan, told the pollsters encouragingly. "Or is it strongly?"

American Heritage
Dictionary—II

English suffers endless indignities, but it does not suffer in silence. So many expressions offend against hearing, taste or intelligence that linguistic vigilantes are forever deploying the weapons of authority, scorn, imprecation, even despair. A few of the critics manage to keep their powder wry.

About a dozen years ago, the publishers of *The American Heritage Dictionary*, seeking protection in numbers, collected a posse entitled "Usage Panel." Houghton Mifflin, the Boston publisher which now rides herd over the dictionary, eventually enlarged that posse by about a third—to roughly 150 deputies—and named Edwin Newman leader of the vigilantes.

Summoned via mailed ballot to examine the latest atrocities, the deputies fired away.

Would you favor "affordables," as in "determining the affordables of skilled workers in a time of prosperity"?

Robert Coughlan, author: "This jars my ear but it is useful; so, reluctantly, yes."

Heywood Hale Broun, interviewer: "Should be limited

to use in those TV commercials which suggest that some vulgar extravagance is within your reach."

Orville Prescott, author: "Vile!"

Isaac Asimov, author: "Ugly word. I have negatived its advisables."

Red Smith, columnist: "The mother tongue can't afford it."

Annie Dillard, author: "Egad."

"Admit" (in the sense of "confess" or "acknowledge") is often used with "to," as in "She admitted to having withheld information." Acceptable?

Gilbert Highet, editor: "Negative. American English tends to heap up unnecessary prepositions and prepositional adverbs: students don't study Aristotle, they study UP ON Aristotle; people don't meet friends, they meet UP WITH friends. The 'to' is quite otiose."

Russell Baker, columnist: "Usage has triumphed on this one. (Question: Why is it 'usage,' not 'use'?)"

What about "cost out," as in "the procedure for costing out a proposal?"

Heywood Hale Broun: "Perhaps acceptable among accountants but not for use in normal speech or writing."

Isaac Asimov: "I have considered this and valued out the phrase."

Robert Coughlan: "Vulgar, meager, lamebrained."

Annie Dillard: "No nay never."

Would you accept "downplay" as transitive verb and as noun, as in "The delegate downplayed the reported anxiety over the party's abortion plank" and "The Russians quietly shelved a campaign to convene a new conference, and press treatment of such a meeting reflects the downplay"?

Gilbert Highet, yea-saying to the verb form: "I think

this is acceptable: we have a downcast and downweigh. My wife, Helen MacInnes, disagrees and considers it a detestable formation."

Winthrop Sargeant, author, saying no: "Too many *good* synonyms: minimize, disparage, discount, belittle, doubt the importance of, call in question, etc., etc."

David Ogilvy, advertising executive: "Should be played down."

Jacques Barzun, author: "What's wrong with 'played down'? Shall we be saying 'The defeated candidate ingave'?"

Peter De Vries, author: "If I heard a speaker use it I would upget and outwalk."

Robert Coughlan: "Revolting."

Is it acceptable to use "free up," as in "a new copying machine that will free up your secretary"?

J.K. Galbraith, economist: "Indecent, even obscene."

Jacques Barzun: "She's a loose woman already."

Nat Hentoff, author: "I think there's a chance of nipping this one. It should be shunned up."

Was it acceptable to write that "She gaveled the convention to order"?

Sheridan Baker, English professor: "...and hammered home her plank?"

Jacques Barzun: "...and waterglassed the final remarks, I suppose."

Annie Dillard, voting yes: "This is no different from axing a tree."

John Ciardi, poet: "Why not? Compared to 'called' it is a precision."

Heywood Hale Broun: "If it's actually on schedule you may use any word you want as a reward."

Vermont Royster, former editor, voting no: "She called

the convention to order—with or without a gavel."

Peter De Vries: "It gravels me."

Robert Coughlan: "Ugh!"

Is "gay" (homosexual) as an adjective and as a noun appropriate to formal speech and writing? How about "gays" as in "The gays were among small groups of protesters"?

Annie Dillard, voting yes for "gay": "If that's what they want, let them have it—as an adjective..."

Ken McCormick, editor, voting yes for "gay": "In one short word it says a lot." Voting no for "gays": "Inconsistently, I don't like 'gays.' "

Sheridan Baker: "Yes—even though I must register as a morose."

Arthur M. Schlesinger Jr., historian: " 'Gay' used to be one of the most agreeable words in the language. Its appropriation by a notably morose group is an act of piracy."

Gilbert Highet: "Auden was a very amusing man when slightly drunk, but one look at that seamed and haggard face would keep anyone from calling him GAY."

Isaac Asimov: "I bitterly resent the manner in which 'gay' has been forced out of speech. I can no longer say, 'I feel gay' or speak of a 'gay spirit.' "

Russell Baker: "The current acceptance of 'gay' reflects a modern tendency of educated folk to oblige vociferously aggrieved minorities too readily, sometimes with odious results."

Nat Hentoff: "I would prefer 'gayim' (as in 'goyim'), with no pejorative meaning intended."

"Input" is used as equivalent to "data or information" in charting a course, as in "The President had access to varied input," and to "an active role" as in "The nominee declared that he had no input in adoption of the plank." Yes or no?

Jacques Barzun: "...jargon—and very vague, since input can mean anything from a Congressional appropriation to a frankfurter at lunch."

Nat Hentoff: "...mechanical shorthand that rusts thought."

Bruce Catton, historian: "...particularly offensive form of the Social Science jargon."

John Fowles, author: "A Watergatism (mechanistic barbarism)!"

Lewis Mumford, author: "'Input' has a legitimate use in computerdom—otherwise it should be shunned. It is the equivalent of 'y'know' for those who don't know the right word."

Berton Roueché, author: "I accept 'output,' but—I don't know why—'input' turns my stomach. Maybe it's the people who use such words."

Pierre Berton, author: "I do not mingle socially with people who talk this way and would not expect my readers to stick with me if I used it."

Reuven Frank, television producer, voting no: "If there is output there must be input. If there is outcry there must be incry. If there is outlaw there must be inlaw. So the reasoning is junk."

Gilbert Highet: "...carries an objectionable image of a politician as a sort of IBM machine passively receiving whatever people stuff into his slots."

Peter De Vries: "...the thought of putting information into a President is a little grotesque."

Red Smith: "This usage brings a violent output of nausea here. Couldn't the President have access to advice instead?"

Is it acceptable "to make a keynote address"?

Heywood Hale Broun: "Why not? A vague word for a vague performance."

Gilbert Highet: "Negative, because one can keynote a meeting in various ways—e.g. by devoting most of the agenda to one subject, by draping the hall in black, by staging a mock assassination during the first session."

Powerbroker, or even power broker?

Peter De Vries: "An adroit coinage, but will probably turn out to be one of those tendentious words that proliferate the reality they presume to denote, so that soon we shall have powerbrokers under every bed just as now we have the establishment lurking in every corner."

Eugene J. McCarthy, former Senator: "It doesn't describe—either political reality or the function of a broker."

"Prioritize," as in "a first attempt to prioritize the tasks facing the new administration"?

Eugene J. McCarthy: "Neither first Priorities nor (a la J. Carter) last Priority."

Lewis Mumford: "Imitation academic gobbledygook."

J.K. Galbraith: "Terrible. Also cannot be spoken."

Peter De Vries: "The language is already cacophonized enough."

Paul Horgan, author: "Anyone who would accept this must surely have a 'tin ear.' "

Heywood Hale Broun: "I'm afraid this one head-acheizes me too much for sensible comment."

Red Smith: "Let's negatize this one, wordwise."

Jessica Mitford, author: "No, no, no, PLEASE!!"

Is "target" as a verb meaning "to make a target of," as in "Republican convention speakers targeted the Democratic nominee" acceptable in current usage?

Isaac Asimov: "Hate it. Bureaucratese."

John Ciardi: "Federalese."

Russell Baker: "...Pentagonese. Are we all going to start writing like a building?"

The administration's decision was to tilt toward Pakistan in the conflict with India. Is "tilt" acceptable?

Shana Alexander: "ᵀ find it imaginative and graphic (although sinister)."

Isaac Asimov: "...an unpleasant reminder of the Nixon days."

Theodore C. Sorensen, lawyer and former CIA director-designate: "Yes."

The broadest approval—84 per cent—went to *power-broker* or *power broker*. A majority of panelists rejected almost all other usages proposed. The lowest vote of approval was for *prioritize*—three per cent.

Senator Mark Hatfield, eager not to offend, or simply not offended, voted the straight permissive ticket, accepting all the uses colleagues found abhorrent or incredible.

Paul Theroux, author: "This questionnaire offers the clearest proof imaginable that the political process is damaging to the linguistic health of our country."

Heywood Hale Broun: "Pericles, Cicero, Burke, and Lincoln were politicians and they didn't talk or write this way. What happened?"

Wallace Stegner: "Most of these make me faintly ill. I'm glad I'm getting old."

Barbara W. Tuchman, historian: "I consider this whole list an absurdity—and an insult to the purpose of maintaining the structure and grammar of the English language, not to mention the goals of education. To give such usages the dignity of even asking whether they are acceptable is to partake in this wrecking of the English language."

Harper Dictionary of Contemporary Usage

In 1971, William and Mary Morris, editors of the *Harper Dictionary of Contemporary Usage*, began sending questionnaires on usage to those they describe as "distinguished literary figures, commentators and language experts." Since, as the Morrises maintain, "the day when one person...could dictate the rights and wrongs of language are long past," they consulted 136 experts. All of them have been known to wag pen and tongue, and they handed down opinions with the aplomb of a Supreme Court Justice (one—William O. Douglas, *was* a Supreme Court Justice) or at least of an avenging angel. Occasionally these unpaid verdicts seem to come not from what the Morrises describe as a cross section, but from a cross section.

Noted Abe Burrows, who has spent a lifetime at the bedside of ailing lines: "Those wicked criminals who commit high crimes against grammar, i.e. saying 'between you and I' or 'He invited she and I to a party,' shall have an evil spell cast over 'they' for all their miserable lives."

"Homer distinguished between winged and unwinged words," insisted Erich Segal, the classicist and marathon runner. "So should we. Dammit."

Rex Stout, the mystery writer, fulminated that changes "imposed by ignorant clowns such as advertising copywriters and broadcasters are abominable and should be condemned by all lovers of language."

To wit:

Do panelists observe the distinction between "admittance to the theater" and "admission of guilt?"

Shana Alexander, columnist: "No, but I will from now on."

Edwin Newman, author of "Strictly Speaking": "No—but I should."

Vermont Royster, columnist: "No—and I know no one who does."

Red Smith, columnist: "Yes. Of course—unless we're talking Swahili."

Would you accept "I ain't the least bit interested"?

John Ciardi, poet: "'Ain't' is the right and inevitable contraction the language demands and will have. No amount of schoolmarming will suppress it."

Dwight MacDonald, critic, voting no: "Alas, the 19th-century schoolmarms did their work so well."

Wright Morris, novelist: "'Ain't' is an ugly sound and we should preserve it *as* ugly."

May "alibi" be used for any kind of excuse?

Anthony Burgess, author: "'Alibi' means 'somewhere else' to me. It can't mean one thing in Latin and law and another thing in nonlegal English."

Justice Douglas: "'Yes' to the use of alibi in the extended sense, both in speech and writing."

May "author" be a verb?

Saul Bellow, author: "No, nor the word 'crafted.' Abominable!"

Herman Wouk, author: "No, no, no, no, no, no, no! NO!"

Do you accept "between you and I" in casual speech?

Berton Roueché, writer, voting no: "Why should error be approved?"

Geoffrey Hellman, author, voting yes: "Upper-class affectation. Maybe lower-class too, but I don't know the lower classes."

An editor visited a journalism school and "critiqued" the college paper. Would you approve this use of "critique" as a transitive verb?

Michael J. Arlen, writer: "It sounds stupid."

Mr. Burgess: "No, no. A critique is like what Kant wrote about pure reason."

Stanley Kunitz, poet: "Dreadful!"

Barbara Tuchman, historian: "If there is such a school, its license should be taken away."

Mr. Wouk: "Yecch!"

The suffix –ee is widely used, as in draftee and trainee. What about standee and escapee?

Isaac Asimov, the writer: "As a writee, why not?"

Mr. Burrows: "If a show of mine has 'standees' I enjoy the bad grammar."

May critics enthuse over a play?

Mr. Burrows: "The critics 'enthuse' so rarely that I should welcome the word. But I don't like it."

Charles Kuralt, of TV: "...but the audience 'apathied' over it? Lord, no. A terrible word."

Mr. Wouk: "This one is making it, I believe."

Would you approve "The committee met to finalize plans for the dinner"?

Walter Cronkite: "A valuable new form."

Mr. Kuralt: "It's a Washington word. The Washington

example has very often served to bastardize (to use a non-Washington word) the language these last 20 years, with the connivance, alas, of reporters in Washington, who should know better."

Lionel Trilling, the critic: "In speech, yes—reluctantly—and I would be suspicious of people who used it."

Is there a distinction between flaunt and flout—used interchangeably by two court justices—worth preserving?

Mr. Arlen: "I should damn well hope so."

Ben Lucien Burman, novelist: "No wonder Roosevelt wanted to fire the Supreme Court!"

Mr. Kunitz: "I flout those who flaunt their ignorance."

May graffiti be used as singular, though the singular in Italian is graffito?

Joseph A. Brandt, former editor: "When not in Rome, do as the Americans do."

Robert Crichton, novelist: "I go on the assumption the Italians are wrong."

Peter S. Prescott, critic: "Spaghetti is usually thought of as an undifferentiated mass; not so graffiti, which are often strikingly individual."

May hopefully—which means "full of hope"—be used in "Hopefully, the war will be ended"?

Miss Alexander: "Slack-jawed, common, sleazy."

Leo Rosten, author: "This is simply barbarism. What does 'hopefully' modify. Does a war 'hope'?"

Jean Stafford, author: "On my back door there is a sign with large lettering which reads: 'THE WORD "HOPEFULLY" MUST BE MISUSED ON THESE PREMISES. VIOLATORS WILL BE HUMILIATED.' "

Has the moment come for "irregardless"?

Robert Cromie, TV journalist: "No. I am irrelentless in my opposition."

Alexander Kendrick, correspondent: "Undoubtedly, no."

Wright Morris, novelist: "I say no; my wife says yes."

Are media ever singular? Would you accept "The White House requested the cooperation of all the medias"?

Elizabeth Janeway, writer: "Never Never Never Never Never! (Though I wouldn't be surprised at the White House.)"

Mr. Asimov: "Let's put out a few memorandas on the subject after collecting the necessary datas."

Mr. Cronkite: "Mr. Agnew probably would say: 'The media is all graffiti and they're all obscene—but I wouldn't."

How about highway signs reading "Go Slow" (instead of "Slowly")?

Leon Edel, biographer: "'Slowly' would distract the illiterate."

Leonard Sanders, critic: "Safety first; grammatical considerations second."

Would the panel accept "Performancewise, the new man proved a failure"?

Mr. Cronkite: "A very valuable, meaningful mutation."

Miss Janeway: "No. Yet it has a kind of eerie fascination. I would like to know howwise he proved a success."

Walter Lord, author: "Usagewise, I abhor it."

Russell Lynes, author: "No wise!"

There was doubtful comfort in numbers—even when 136 experts joined to prepare for the worst. Eugene J. McCarthy, the former Senator who speaks with a loud voice quadrennially and in scholarly tones all the time, warned:

"We must now look to new threats, although the Ford Administration [used] metaphors from football and from the furniture business, such as 'the unvarnished facts' and 'Truth is the glue that holds the government together'."

Summing it up Miss Stafford predicted a fate worse than death for the American language. "The tough and dandy darling is going into paresis," she warned, adding: "Do count on me as a dedicated physician who will even pay house calls in the middle of the night."

"A society indifferent to right words is a society grown careless of its lifegiving values," insisted Mr. Kunitz.

Professor Trilling remained in a class of his own. Said he: "I find righteous denunciations of the present state of the language no less dismaying than the present state of the language."

This book was set in Century Expanded
Composed, printed, and bound by the
Mark IV Press, Deer Park, N.Y.

BARNHART BOOKS, PUBLISHERS